PINPOINT OF ETERNITY

European Literature in Search of the All-Encompassing Moment

GERMAN LITERATURE ART & THOUGHT

An International Forum for Interdisciplinary Studies
including

THE McMASTER COLLOQUIUM ON GERMAN LITERATURE

Vols. IIIff, edited by Gerald Chapple and Hans Schulte

General Editor: **Hans Schulte**

Associate Editors: *Peter Heller*
Gerald Chapple

ADVISORY BOARD

PINPOINT OF ETERNITY

European Literature in Search of
the All-Encompassing Moment

Peter Salm

UNIVERSITY
PRESS OF
AMERICA

LANHAM • NEW YORK • LONDON

Co-published by arrangement with
German Literature, Art and Thought, McMaster University

Library of Congress Cataloging in Publication Data

Salm, Peter.
  Pinpoint of eternity.

  (German literature, art, and thought)
  Bibliography: p.
  Includes index.
    1. Time in literature.   2. European literature—
History and criticism.   I. Title.   II. Series.
  PN56.T5S25   1986   809'.93355   85-26643
  ISBN 0-8191-5208-0 (alk. paper)
  ISBN 0-8191-5209-9 (pbk. : alk. paper)

To June,
my incomparable friend, critic, and wife

CONTENTS

PINPOINT
OF
ETERNITY

ACKNOWLEDGMENTS

My involvement with mystical or poetic abrogations of sequential time goes back to 1973 when I wrote an essay with the title "Pinpoint of Eternity: the Sufficient Moment in Literature."[1] Once broached, the topic refused to go away. Examples of "Moments" multiplied when I dipped into almost any phase of European literature of the Christian era. The problem therefore turned out to be not so much how to expand the original essay, but rather how to limit a large quantity of relevant materials, so that a manageable volume might result.

I have had much help, some of it by way of conversations with colleagues. My friend Roger Salomon, Professor of English at Case Western Reserve University, directed my attention to medieval and Renaissance forms of mysticism which during propitious moments of religious insight, would suffuse the day-to-day experience of space and time. Professor Herbert Long, a Greek and Latin scholar also of Case Western, directed my attention to a passage of high poetry in the Gospel of John (John 8.58) where the linearity of human history suddenly lights up in a flashpoint of eternal simultaneity (see p. 24). Peter Heller, Professor of German and Comparative Literature at SUNY, Buffalo, was an early supporter of the manuscript. I was grateful for his suggestions which, I am convinced, served to improve the manuscript. My thanks also go to Professor Hans Schulte, the editor, and to his colleague Gerald Chapple, both of the German Department at McMaster University in Hamilton, Ontario, for thoughtfully steering the manuscript toward publication, with much forbearance of the author's idiosyncracies.

Sharply focused, strenuous discussions, as well as casual conversations in a coffee-shop environment were important preliminaries, and aftermaths, to the clatterings of my dear manual typewriter.

---

[1] Studies in 18th-Century Culture, ed. Harold E. Pagliaro (Cleveland, 1973), pp. 49-65.

INTRODUCTION

> Really, universally, relations stop nowhere, and the
> exquisite problem of the artist is eternally but to draw, by a
> geometry of his own, the circle within which they shall
> happily appear to do so. . . .
> HENRY JAMES, FROM THE PREFACE TO *RODERICK HUDSON*.

Literature is irrevocably a temporal art. The notion that sentences, acts of a drama and entire novels may have — or ought to have — an instantaneous presence in the minds of both the writer and his public, may at first seem strained and quixotic. Yet along with the succession of events which form the skeletal structure of a fiction, it is possible to perceive in it — surrounding and suffusing the chronology — an instantaneous and concentrated form of a meaningful presentness. It is a condition concerning which Frank Kermode in his important book, *The Sense of an Ending*, observed: ". . . in every plot there is an escape from chronicity, a deviation from this norm of reality."[1] Fictions, according to this view, are dominated by their endings which exercise their power in such a way as to bring all events into concordance with them. In the context of the Scriptures, it is the Apocalypse which signals the providential goal of human history, and a general analogy between the Bible and secular writing suggests that literary endings ought to be similarly regarded as non-temporal consummations of a work's temporal progression. In the Scriptures, in fact, the endings of all major episodes are endowed with a double focus: one of them has the sharp outlines of actual, fundamentalist reality; the other is bathed in the light of eternity. The events recounted in this double perspective are therefore not merely successive, but because of their participation in infinity, simultaneous as well. The imminence of an anticipated event becomes the immanence of one event in another. As history the Scriptures are anchored in time,

---

[1] (New York, 1968), p. 50.

and as Divine revelation they are aspects of an eternal present tense. Each new beginning in time is also the figuration of an ending, and each ending is also "merely" a more profound rendering of a beginning. When the view that the Book of Revelation is potentially present in Genesis is carried over into literature — to follow Kermode's suggestion — it can be seen that the beginnings and middles are shaped by the power emanating from the ending. It is a movement of the mind which is the reverse of the forward direction of traditional literary plots.

Kermode's view, to my mind, has contributed significantly to the understanding of chronological and non-temporal aspects of literary texts, though perhaps it may be broadened; for by directing all attention to the ending — or Apocalypse — of the work, the reader's angle of vision is necessarily narrowed, to the detriment of the complexities residing throughout the composition. After all, if the ending is somehow conceived to be co-present with the beginning and the middle, then each moment can be said to represent symbolically the whole work. There is no reason therefore for the moment which chronologically stands at the end to have a greater "presence" than earlier moments in the text.

The desire to be in touch with everything at once may be interpreted — and is so interpreted in this book — as an aspect of what Camus called "the metaphysical demand for unity."[2] It applies equally to reader and author, and because such a desire can be found as much in third century neo-Platonic philosophy as in modern writers like E.M. Forster, Borges and Beckett, it is tempting to see it as arising from an apparently unextinguishable source of energy that would fuse chronologically separate events in human experience into single meaningful wholes.

While my goal has been to secure a point of view from which literary texts would appear in a fresh light, I have not hesitated to cast an occasional glance beyond the confines of literature; indeed our soundings might here and there impinge on a kind of psychological anthropology, if only because the images of unity in their various permutations, and stemming from widely separated historical periods, are likely to have arisen from roughly the same motivating impulse. Consequently, the centuries are not given the attention in this book that would have been their due had they been viewed in the context of an historical approach, and major phases of the Christian era appear as mere perspectival markers in the development of what from our vantage point may be regarded as a single geometric image: the infinite circle and its ubiquitous center.

My speculations regarding the problems surrounding "unity" in literature stem from an earlier preoccupation with Goethe's *Faust* and with

---

[2] In the essay, "Rebellion and Art," in *The Rebel*, trans. Anthony Bower (New York, 1956), p. 253.

attempts to fathom the substance and form of the *Augenblick*, that quint-essential Moment for the sake of which Faust, the restless humanist intellectual, is prepared to risk eternal damnation. The terms of the Faustian wager conjure up a compelling vision of a pinpoint of time in which all experience is gathered up in an unmediated and simultaneous presentness. The hubris of the hero's ambition leads to tragedy in the first part of the drama — and to a difficult and ambiguous salvation in *Part II*.

Before the eighteenth century, the concept of an all-encompassing point of time could be found only in explicitly religious texts, so far as I can determine. They appeared either in the context of theological exposition or else in the service of poetic imagery. In both cases, a dimensionless presentness was reserved for the divinity alone. An alliance between theology and meditative poetry developed in an atmosphere of neo-Platonic and hermetic sprituality — resulting in a kind of mysticism that helped the faithful narrow the gap between their imperfect, mortal selves and a perceived unconditional mode of being. The mysteries believed to be associated with numbers and spatial relationships reached learned Christians by way of a resurging Pythagorean tradition, and, in keeping with ancient claims, geometric figures began to be seen as avenues to ultimate truths. And among such figures, a special conception of the circle or sphere began to take hold. Not only was the circumference without beginning or end — and could therefore be made to stand for eternity — but there was, in addition, a reciprocal relationship between the circumference and the center which was thought to be of marvelous import. In the thirteenth century, the image of the circle turned up again in the anonymous and now almost forgotten *Book of Twenty-Four Philosophers*, a treatise which proceeded along syllogistic chains of reasoning to proofs and elucidations of the existence of a Supreme Being. Here a seemingly minor departure from the traditional Plotinian characterization of the circle (the "intelligible" circle of Plotinus became an "infinite" circle in the anonymous tract) proved to be a change of considerable consequence, as we shall see in the second chapter.

By the beginning of the fourteenth century, the circle reached its poetic culmination in Dante's *Divine Comedy*, and while it never again reached comparable grandeur, its transcendent geometry continued to occupy a place in metaphysical systems and to lend itself to poetic imagery.

In the fifteenth century, Cardinal Nicholas de Cusa brought his mathematical brilliance to bear on the circle and put his insights at the service of the Church; his intellectual influence mightily contributed to the aura of confidence surrounding creative spirits of the Renaissance. The leading figures in the fifteenth and sixteenth centuries could now see themselves as centers of an infinite cosmic circle and as such in constant "radial" rapport with the divine circumference.

In the seventeenth century, the long-lasting union between geometry and religion found its last proponent in Pascal, who with the authority of a great mathematician used the sphere as a symbol of cosmic immensity and as an argument in support of his conviction that the human condition — in the absence of Christian faith — was desperate beyond repair.

After Kepler, Pascal and Newton, the mathematical sciences were increasingly perceived by their practitioners as irrelevant to the religious sensibility; but in poetry the circle-and-center survived as an effective symbol and continued to appear in various guises or in abbreviated form. In the sixteenth century Maurice Scève (1501-1563) in France and John of the Cross (1542-1591) in Spain had written verses in which the circle-and-center image appeared in the sense of its peculiar double infinity.[3] In England a hymn by Richard Crashaw (1613-1649) contains the lines:

> All-circling point. All-centring sphear.
> The world's one, round, Aeternall year.[4]

And in Germany, Angelus Silesius (1624-1677) composed the rhymed meditation:

Der Kreiss im Puncte
Als GOtt verborgen lag in eines Mägdeleins Schoss /
Da war es / Da der Punct den Kreiss in sich beschloss.[5]

The Circle in the Point
When GOd lay hidden in a maiden's womb,
The point within itself the circle did enclose.

It is noteworthy that so often in Christian contexts, the notions of infinity and eternity which conjure up a boundless vastness of time and

---

[3] See Georges Poulet, *The Metamorphoses of the Circle*, trans. Carley Dawson and Elliott Colemen (Baltimore, 1966), pp. 2, 13. This important book offers an illuminating history of the role and function of the circle from the Renaissance to T.S. Eliot and Jorge Guillen.

[4] *The Poems of Richard Crashaw*, 2nd ed., L.C. Martin, (London, 1966), p. 255.

[5] Cited from *Das Zeitalter des Barock, Texte und Zeugnisse*, ed. Albrecht Schöne, (Munich, 1963), p. 256. Translation mine.

space, are most effectively represented by their exact opposite: a limitless smallness of time and space. In a metaphysical "shifting of gears," infinity is transferred from the periphery to the center. Here where the words for temporal and spatial concepts enjoy a transcendent synonymity, the separate vocabularies of geometry and religion also merge into one. More strikingly than any other figure, the circle (or sphere) could encompass the paradoxes resulting from the attempts to express the Absolute in human terms. One can go no further in unifying oppositions than through the double infinities of the infinite circle, and it is impossible to conceive of a paradox more extreme than that of the center of an infinite circle encompassing its circumference.

In the *Divine Comedy* the full center-circle image informs all three *cantiche*. In *Faust* and in other works closer to our time, only the center remains, still serving the same basic purposes as its theological ancestors. The *Augenblick* and other temporal pinpoints contain all the polar absolutes that Plotinus, St. Augustine or Angelus Silesius had represented by the complete circular image. It is still the maximum enclosed in the minimum.

With Goethe's drama we are given the first vastly important secular treatment of the Eternal Moment, though the religious import of the quest is easy to see. In European Romanticism, experiments designed to overcome the one-thing-after-another nature of storytelling began to appear on the literary scene, and in the twentieth century, the deployment of techniques and stylistic modalities to achieve intimations of simultaneity have become an important and even fashionable concern to writers and critics alike.

The assertion — no matter how tentatively made — that the same source of energy should have fueled great works associated with vastly different periods of European literature runs a double risk: either the claim is too general to have any useful application to particular texts, or else, if it is specific, it may apply to some works and not to others. In order to reduce that risk I have endeavored to let a few major authors speak to that point, one from the waning Middle Ages, another bridging the end of the eighteenth and the beginning of the nineteenth centuries, and two from the first half of this century. The very fact that they can be shown to share certain characteristics in the matter of attempted abrogations of chronicity, even though far apart in their religious and philosophic outlook, has given me courage to argue that perhaps a form of temporal transcendence — some vision of a convergence of time in the present — may be part and parcel of the literary impulse itself.

Georges Poulet showed that all definitions of eternity "conjoin with two terms which are contradictory . . . that only the divine life can reconcile,"[6] and when we in turn think of "the eternal moment," "the

---

[6] Poulet, *Metamorphoses* , p. xii.

maximum in the minimum," or "the all-encompassing center" — to mention only a few such expressions — it can be verified that the closest possible pairing of extreme polarities is their constant characteristic. While it is indisputable that the reconciliation of such polarities is beyond human reach, the attempt to achieve it is the substance of many religious and poetic endeavors.

Poetry is, after all, based on such a paradox. It is rightly considered to be both concrete and universal, or in Hegel's words, alluding to the same condition, "the sensuous radiance of the idea."[7] The concrete plot evolved in time, while the meaning, or "the universal," exists outside of time. As meaning and fictional fact at any juncture seem to merge and to form a new amalgam, we conventionally speak of poetic imagination, or even inspiration. Ideally, every significant moment in a poetic work should be a kind of "center," symbolically containing the whole of the composition. Neither the beginning nor the ending are more important to the literary meaning than the nodal points in between.

Finally, because it is rationally impossible to reconcile the concrete with the universal, literature itself is "impossible." An image which symbolically unites within itself the temporal flow of a narrative — say the madeleine of Proust's *A la recherche du temps perdu* — and in an instant of time radiates the entire novel's meaning, such an image can be seen as a counterpart and analogue to the center which encompasses the circle. Its very impossibility — along with its persuasiveness — constitutes an aspect of its literary value. The pure and all-containing distillate is an ideal which must be forever out of reach, and as the hopelessness of the quest for it becomes — paradoxically — an essential part of the poet's unifying and time-abrogating imagination, literature takes on the stance and style which we associate with the most important works of the twentieth century.

I have devoted separate chapters to Dante, Goethe, Virginia Woolf and Thomas Mann, in order to provide a sampling from different genres and from widely separate phases of European literary history. These particular writers were chosen not only because they were great artificers of "moments" — others with equally impressive and pertinent credentials might have been brought forward — but it was Dante, Goethe and the others who most forcibly brought me face to face with the particular aspect of literary temporality with which I became preoccupied. And it seemed therefore appropriate — the personal element in the choice may be forgiven me — that these four names should take up a dominant position in this volume.

---

7 "Das Schöne bestimmt sich durch das sinnliche Scheinen der Idee . . . ," *Jubiläumsausgabe* (Stuttgart 1964), XII, 160.

Chapter One

BEGINNINGS, MIDDLES AND ENDINGS

> It is not that we are connoisseurs of chaos, but that we are
> surrounded by it, and equipped to coexist with it only by
> our fictive powers.
>
> FRANK KERMODE, *THE SENSE OF AN ENDING*

We need to envision, for the sake of clarity, the relevant theoretical absolutes beyond the ken of literature. Pure successiveness would then be a mere compilation of data arranged in temporal contiguousness, such as a calendar in which various unrelated events are recorded. At the other extreme lie non-temporal concepts, absolute ideas untainted by the intrusion of actuality: brotherly love, the second law of thermodynamics, patriotism. Neither extreme is "literature," but each of them is a significant component of it. A poetic work, then, may be defined as a fusion of a particular sequence of time- and space-bound events with a vital idea or concept which by some alchemy arises from that sequence. Neither the concept nor the story exists as a separate entity outside the confines of the work. The plot shapes itself according to an idea, and conversely the idea emerges from the patterning of the events which make up the plot. For this reason alone, neither a plot summary nor a description of the idea "behind" the work can properly convey its meaning. The epigrammatic observation at the end of Archibald MacLeish's poem "Ars Poetica" that "A poem should not mean but be" is a precise evocation of the ideal of poetry. The successful joining of the polarities — of the particular and the universal of time and non-time — results in a category of human endeavor which is not quite science or philosophy, and never quite a case history, but art.

A literary work, regardless of its genre, may tend toward one or the other. It is obviously useful to be aware, say, of the relative dominance of the "timeless" theme of spurned love in Racine's tragedy *Phèdre*, and by contrast, of the rather self-sufficient presence of a story like Maupassant's *Necklace* in its particular rhythmic progression. Such variations suggest that it should be possible to rough out a general topology of literature in which the relative stress on, as well as the relationship between, the general and the particular would be at the focus of interest. A sensibility prevalent at a particular time and in a culturally coherent region suffuses and often dominates compositional styles. A story to be read, a drama to be heard and seen, may be inhabited by characters who are representative of a type rather than idosyncratic personages. They in turn will activate a plot which suitably exemplifies well-established abstraction, usually in the form of moral principles.

Seventeenth-century France preeminently produced such an idea-dominated literature, and so did the Augustan writers in England. Theoretical manifestos of the time served to justify such idealistic poetic art and provided its practitioners with a sense of tradition rooted in Horatian poetic principles and Roman civic virtues. Echoes of "la belle nature" in Boileau's *Art poétique* can be heard in Pope, Samuel Johnson and Joshua Reynolds. Certainly, the view expressed by Pope in his *Essay on Criticism* that certain time-honored poetic principles — the principles of Neoclasscism — were "discovered, not devised," and represented the world not in the raw but as "nature methodised," was in harmony with his genius for felicitous and persuasive generalization. Another *locus neoclassicus* is a passage in Samuel Johnson's *Rasselas*, where the learned poet Imlac instructs his princely companion: "The business of the poet is to examine, not the individual but the species; . . . he does not number the streaks in the tulip . . . he must neglect the minor discriminations. . . ." And Joshua Reynolds held up to the assembled members of the British Royal Academy the ideals of Neoclassicism when — even in its fading years — he advocated the imitation of "the general idea of nature," and "only what is truly nature," in his *Seventh Discourse*.

As may be expected, the opposite tendency — a predilection for particularity — constitutes a major component of Romantic writings, for example in works by poets such as Wordsworth, Keats, Heine and Leopardi, though to others it was, on the contrary, the luminous abstractions to be found in Novalis, Hölderlin and Shelley that were quintessentially Romantic. Blake's temperament was so constituted that it prompted him to reject the ideal of generalized nature as formulated by Joshua Reynolds. In the *Annotations* of 1808 to Reynolds' *Second Discourse*, he vehemently insisted on the need to "particularise."

To Generalise is to be an Idiot. To particularise is the Alone Distinction of Merit. General Knowledges are those that Idiots possess.[1]

On the other hand, several passages in Shelley's *Defence of Poetry* point to the poet's penchant for majestic concepts, both in content and in the very poetry of the *Defence*: "All high poetry is infinite. . . ." "A poem is the image of life expressed in its eternal truth. . . ." "We want the creative faculty to imagine that which we know. . . ."
It should be easy to see from this that the particular movement from "classical" to "romantic," in either the historical or typological sense, need not coincide with alternations between "abstract" and "concrete" poetry.

It appears that the twentieth century has until now shown itself to be most hospitable to the rendering of objects, phenomena, or imaginary significations, in their concrete particularity. It was the young English philosopher and essayist T.E. Hulme (1883-1917) who, in staking out his own anti-Romantic position, influenced T.S. Eliot and accurately predicted the dominant tendency of poetry after the first World War. A summarizing passage of his essay "Romanticism and Classicism," written only a short time before he was killed in the trenches, reads as follows:

> The great aim is accurate, precise, and definite description . . . I can now get at the positive fundamental quality of verse which constitutes excellence, which has nothing to do with infinity, with mystery or with emotions.
> This is the point I aim at, then, in my argument. I prophesy that a period of dry, hard, classical verse is coming.[2]

Statements like these serve to convey the range of the spectrum extending between concreteness on one side and abstraction on the other. An historical study of theoretical positions relevant to this matter and of the literary practices in which they are reflected (or from a different vantage point: of theoretical positions provoked by already existing practices) might provide some insight into the alternation of important modalities of poetic expression. An investigation along these lines could provide a valuable complement to the traditional movements seen traversing and dividing the history of literature.

However, our interest in this exploration is not directed toward historical developments, but rather toward the problems posed by literary

---

[1] *The Complete Writings of William Blake*, ed. Geoffrey Keynes (London, 1964), p. 451.

[2] T.E. Hulme, *Speculations: Essays on Humanism and the Philosophy of Art*, ed. Herbert Read (London, 1954), pp. 133-134.

beginnings and endings which are relevant to all poetic writing, no matter when it was sung or penned, because behind poetic coherences there seems to lie a remarkably stable configuration or image, from which literary productions draw their integrating energies. The conformation and function of such coherences, their kinship to religious mysticism, seem to me to constitute large, distinct and most rewarding objects of investigation.

It should be made clear, if only to avoid misunderstanding, that an author's predilection for either abstract or concretely particular imagery in no way touches on that quality of poetic composition which induces the reader, or spectator, to translate what he has experienced into something of universal significance. Such an effect cannot be attached to one or the other stylistic tendency. That is after all the measure of a work's capacity to engrave itself upon the reader's consciousness. Certainly the precise verbal rendering of significant detail in Flaubert's *Madame Bovary* is fully as capable of conjuring up universal meanings as the explicitly stated moral and religious principles which inform Dostoevski's *Crime and Punishment*, a novel in which little attention is given to the details of the characters' personal appearance. Nor does Antigone, in Sophocles' tragedy, have any prescribed physical features except for those commonly associated with youth and femininity. Her mere presence — even when her face is hidden behind a conventional theatrical mask — embodies the principle for which she suffers and dies. On the other hand, Ibsen's Hedda Gabler is a character who unmistakably belongs to a particular time and place. The play contains elaborate instructions concerning furniture and decor, as we can see by the stage direction accompanying her first entrance:

> Hedda enters the rear room from the left, and comes into the drawing room. She is a woman of twenty-nine. Distinguished, aristocratic face and figure. Her complexion is pale and opalescent. Her eyes are steel-grey, with an expression of cold, calm serenity. Her hair is of handsome auburn colour, but is not especially abundant. She is dressed in an elegant, somewhat loose-fitting morning gown.[3]

Time and space in *Antigone* are vague and infused with the mythological past. The tragedy's formal severity points to its origin in religious ritual, while in *Hedda Gabler*, Ibsen's obsessive attention to the details of a late-nineteenth-century, upper-class, Scandinavian home, are in conformity with the scientific and psychological objectivity demanded by the canons of Naturalism. Yet in spite of the enormous gulf between these two representations of life, they are both poetry — in the sense

---

[3] Michael Meyer, trans. (New York: Anchor Books, 1961), p. 286.

of *Dichtung* — and as poetry they necessarily partake of concreteness and universality. The predominance of one — say the insistence on particularity — over the other creates an interesting tilt in the balance, but the annihilation of one by the other would necessarily also annihilate the work's standing as literature. When the boundaries of the spectrum in whose range imaginary writing can flourish are violated, the writer may find himself in the territory of philosophical exposition, or — having crossed the opposite frontier — in that of journalistic reportage. The necessary conditions for the quality of "literariness" were sketched out by W.K. Wimsatt in his essay "The Concrete Universal," first published in 1947:

> Whether or not one believes in universals, one may see the presence in literary criticism of a theory that poetry presents the concrete and the universal, or the individual and the universal, or an object which in a mysterious and special way is both highly general and highly particular.[4]

To see a work of literature as a fusion of such opposites involves a circular kind of reasoning: a series of facts and events present themselves as standing for some meaning or concept — say, one having to do with love of one's country, or hatred of treachery — while the literary presence of the idea emerges only when all the facts of the plot have come to the fore. The futility of any attempt to fathom the initial creative impulse is evident enough. What is important and what needs to be acknowledged is that neither the conceptual nor the factual aspects are stabilized until the process of artistic creation — and indeed the reader's empathic re-creation — have reached a modicum of completeness. It is a productive circularity, the hermeneutic circle par excellence, which is not vicious, but a necessary condition for creative activity.[5]

The critical comments which are lavished upon great works of literature invariably probe for some central meaning, only to find that this meaning is so enmeshed in its verbal, tonal and rhythmic texture that it cannot be isolated without violating its integrity. If on the other hand it were possible to avoid any reference to an overall meaning — to bracket out any notion of the meaning, say, of Homer's *Iliad* — then each of the many isolated contingencies would be deprived of the aesthetic value with which it is endowed by the context.

At the heart of the Concrete Universal is its paradoxical nature. Hegel effectively pointed to it and also mirrored it by his shrewd use of an

---

[4] *PMLA*, 62 (March 1947), 262; also in *The Verbal Icon* (New York 1958), p. 71.
[5] See also Heidegger, *Sein und Zeit* (Halle 1929), p. 153; Wellek and Warren, *Theory of Literature*, 2nd ed. (New York 1956), p. 247.

oxymoron when he referred to the aesthetic object as the "sensuous radiance of the idea," a characterization which would be equally apt — though quite un-Hegelian — if it were inverted to read "the ideational radiance of the concrete particular." Such an inversion would result from a small shift in the observer's sense of primacy with respect to the same phenomenon.

We can now begin to see a structural analogy between concrete universality on the one hand, and the notion of literary beginnings and endings on the other, and note that the latter, which provides closures to "meaningful" sequences, has no objective existence outside the text. What one person experiences as a beginning in an uninterrupted flow of non-imagined events, the other may hold to be a middle or an ending. Only the imaginative process — the poetic activity which can somehow transcend the paradox of concrete universality — will give coherence and unity to otherwise merely contingent events.

Aristotle's descriptive definitions are of little help here. The "beginnings, middles and end" which he discerns in tragedy — and also in Homer's *Iliad* and *Odyssey* — somehow continue to seem plausible to the modern student, although the use of "logic" or "necessity" as delimiting elements are no longer satisfying. "A beginning is that," we read in Butcher's translation of the seventh chapter of the *Poetics*, "which does not itself follow anything by causal necessity, but after which something naturally comes to be." And by analogous reasoning, Aristotle maintains that an end is "that which itself naturally follows some other thing, either by necessity or as a rule, but has nothing following it."

The bracketing of the unceasing flow of events into discrete "actions" which are available for "imitation" by the literary artist, can in our time no longer be grounded in Aristotelian logic or necessity. Still, we tend to live at peace with the notion that life can be seen as a series of plots, just as in a spatial context we accept the organization of the night-sky into convenient patterns like the Big Dipper, or Cassiopeia, or Orion, in full knowledge that these images, deeply imbedded in language and culture, are obsolete in the light of modern astronomy. Indeed, the grouping of real or imagined phenomena in conformity with traditional paradigms, appears to satisfy a basic condition of experience and is symptomatic of man's creative rapport with his environment. Chaos is intolerable. Even the ticking of a clock is converted into a schema for rudimentary plots as a number of "perceived presents," between a "tick" at the beginning, and a "tock" at the end. Each tick-tock appears to us naturally as a discrete unit.[6] Thus the imaginative faculty, as well as convention, will relate events in time and objects in space, and in

---

[6] See Paul Fraisse, *The Psychology of Time* (New York, 1963), pp. 77, 84-85.

doing so arrange, select, and even see them in such a way as to make them con-form. "It is not that we are connoisseurs of chaos," Kermode wrote in regard to narrative prose, "but that we are surrounded by it and equipped for coexistence with it only by our fictive powers."[7]

Near the turn of the eighteenth century, Goethe had perceived the problem as relevant not only to poetry but also to his endeavors as a natural philosopher. In his synthesizing efforts in the field of biology he was driven to the edge of despair by what struck him as an unresolvable polar opposition between his observations of natural phenomena on the one hand, and an idea, or conception, that could account for them. The gulf between the two — as he somewhat diffidently hinted in the passage cited here — could be overcome only by an integrating poetic activity:

> Reason cannot bring together what the senses have delivered to it separately, and so the quarrel between sense perception and abstraction remains forever unresolved.
> Hence we take some pleasure in making our escape into poetry. . . .[8]

Perhaps Goethe found himself treading on the ground just this side of the Nothingness which a century and a half later engulfed Jean Paul Sartre's hero Roquentin, in *Nausea*. In this novel, the citizens of Bouville live their lives according to the roles which cling to them like garments and which help them avoid a face-to-face encounter with their undefined selves. The portrait in oil of Pacôme, once a leading citizen of Bouville, most clearly shows the imprint of a life defined from without. Walking through the town's art gallery, Roquentin muses about this imposing personality, this framed countenance gazing down from high on the wall:

> *Pacôme* never made a mistake. He had always done his duty, all his duty, his duty as son, husband, father, leader. . . .
> He had never looked further into himself: he was a leader.[9]

Roquentin finds the chink in the armor of his own role-playing *pour-soi*. When the notion of an "adventure" had first occurred to him, he had thought of it as tantamount to the performance of spectacular deeds in exotic circumstances. Now he knows that an adventure is an experience of coherence and unity, a psychologically beneficent deception:

> This feeling of adventure definitely does not come from events: I have proved it. It's rather the way in which the moments are linked together. I think this

---

[7] *Sense of an Ending*, p. 64.
[8] *Goethes Werke*, Hamburger Ausgabe (Hamburg, 1955), XIII, 32. Translation mine.
[9] Jean-Paul Sartre, *Nausea*, trans. Lloyd Alexander (New York, 1964), pp. 84-85.

is what happens: you suddenly feel that time is passing, that each instant leads to another, this one to another one, and so on; that each instant is annihilated, that it isn't worthwhile to hold it back. . . . And then you attribute this property to events which appear to you in the instants; what belongs to the form you carry over into the content.[10]

Here recollected experience and an important element of poetic creativity appear to be at one. Only that which in the instant of remembrance radiates — to use Kermode's expression — a "sense of an ending" can fit into the particular coherence of a literary work. The sense of a beginning is implied and that of an "adventure" supplies the illusion of meaning. Indeed, near the end of the novel, struggling to overcome his nausea, Roquentin abandons his labors which were to culminate in a historical biography of a major personage from Bouville, named Rollebon, a task on which he had lavished years of diligent effort. It did not come together and he therefore resolves to compose "a story . . . something that could never happen, an adventure."[11]

Poetic "making" has passed through numerous interpretations, ranging from skill and craftsmanship to a mediated transmittal of divine wisdom. Part of the creative process, no doubt, is the selection and organization of materials that will go into the "idea" of a finished work. The subtle forces governing this process are memorably conveyed by Henry James in a passage from the Preface to his first novel, *Roderick Hudson* (1875):

Really, universally, relations stop nowhere, and the exquisite problem of the artist is eternally but to draw, by a geometry of his own, the circle within which they shall happily *appear* to do so . . . the fascination resides . . . in the presumability *somewhere* of a convenient, of a visibly appointed stopping-place. Art would be easy indeed if, by a fond power disposed to patronize it, such conveniences, such simplifications, had been provided. We have, as the case stands, to invent and establish them. . . . The very meaning of expertness is acquired courage to brace one's self for the cruel crisis from the moment one sees it grimly loom.[12]

Behind such observations, it seems to me, lies the Hegelian "sensuous radiance of the idea," the impossible aesthetic fusion which was invoked by Coleridge when he spoke of the "union and interpenetration of the universal and the particular" in the dramas of Shakespeare; and by Wordsworth in the *Essay, Supplementary to the Preface of the Lyrical*

---

[10] *Ibid.*, p. 56.
[11] Ibid., p. 178.
[12] *The Novels of Henry James*, New York edition (New York: Scribner's, n.d.), I, VII-VIII.

Ballads (1815), where he speaks of poetry which, while "ethereal and transcendent," owes its existence as poetry to "sensuous incarnation." More recently, Camus acknowledged his own debt to German idealism in the essay "Rebellion and Art," when he wrote that "art realizes, without apparent effort, the reconciliation of the unique with the universal of which Hegel dreamed."

One suspects that it is not creative artists alone who are confronted with the necessity for such a reconciliation. The imagination is capable of energizing adventures in language, regardless of the speaker's or writer's profession. There is no reason to doubt that the most casual conversational moment may harbor an original vision endowed with a quality which we have good reason to associate with poetry. The person who invented the phrase "my heart goes out to you" rendered his compassion poetically, and whoever it was who first thought of saying "he bit off more than he could chew," created a poetic metaphor for a well-known, unpleasant predicament. To be sure, such phrases are not poems but discrete images which are characteristically "poetic." The power to formulate such Concrete Universals, to relate them to one another as constituent parts of a larger, more complex and more encompassing metaphor, is the special gift of creative writers.

The discovery of the common principles underlying everyday speech and the language of poetry belongs above all to Romanticism. Shelley was one of those who believed in such a shared origin, as can be seen in a passage from the *Defence* where, as elsewhere in the essay, abstract thoughts have a way of glowing from within luminous poetic imagery:

> In the infancy of society every author is necessarily a poet, because language is itself poetry. . . . Every original language near to its source is in itself the chaos of a cyclic poem: the copiousness of lexicography and the distinctions of grammar are the works of a later age, and are merely the catalogue of the form of the creations of poetry.

And it should not be forgotten that before Shelley, Giambattista Vico early in the eighteenth century, and Herder in its closing decades in Germany, had already formulated a theory — through logical argument and through rhapsodic assertion respectively, that the beginnings of language and the creation of poetry, in the sense of *Dichtung*, were closely analogous with regard to their underlying impulses and also with regard to their verbal imagery.

With modern literary theory we appear to have come full circle. In the course of evaluating the impact on American criticism of methods developed in France during the decades following World War II and subsumed under the name of Structuralism, Geoffrey Hartman speculates that "Grammar, language and poetry . . . might . . . be looked at

. . . as a second power of naming. We could think of literature as a
hoard of sacred and magical words that the poet, as secular priest, makes
available."[13] A Novalis and a Shelley might well have applauded such
a statement.

In poetry, the fusion of a concretely temporal component with what
is abstract and non-temporal, must always be less than perfect, but the
implicit goal of perfection creates tensions between the polarities which
can be experienced as aesthetically valuable. A literary text has meaning,
even if it is a representation of meaninglessness, of absurdity, or of life
as a chaos of aleatory contingencies. Even here the successiveness of
words, phrases and paragraphs are permeated by the overriding, non-
successive and non-temporal sense of their meaninglessness. The
unremitting futilites enacted between Estragon, Vladimir and Pozzo in
Samuel Beckett's *Waiting for Godot*, the monotonous rhythms in the
lives of these characters, have become a paradigm of the human predicament. Here the present plagiarizes the past. Intimations of paralysis
in the repetition of phrases such as "there's nothing to be done" and
"it's inevitable" inform the play like provisional summaries of nothingness, and the ending — in the form of a final stage direction — is a
marker toward future inaction: "They do not move." Despite all this,
Waiting for Godot is a marvelously meaningful metaphor which unfolds
between a beginning and an ending. And when pressed for an answer
to the question "a metaphor for what?", one might offer something like
"waitful paralysis" as one of numerous alternatives, so long as it is
understood that the only adequate answer would be tautologically the
play itself in its entirety, even though for those who "know" the play,
its meaning can become manifest in an instant of retrospective consciousness. To attribute an overall coherence to the events enacted in
the play is one way of demonstrating the well-known truth that a ni-
hilistic play, or novel, or poem, is a contradiction in terms.

To ask what a work of literature is "about" is a challenge that should
lead to an encounter with its center. Sometimes the author will be help-
ful by supplying a revealing title like "The Wasteland," or "A la
recherche du temps perdu," but more often one must rely on the totality
of the text to reveal a central meaning. Goethe's *Faust* and Tolstoy's
Anna Karenina are after all only names, and useless as such in the quest
for the meaning of the work to which they provide the title, though it
is undoubtedly true that, in retrospect, it is difficult to utter them without at the same time evoking their Goethean or Tolstoyan context.

---

[13] "Structuralism: The Anglo-American Adventure," *Yale French Studies* (October, 1966), p. 149.

Sometimes the touchstone of meaning can be found in a single ruling image. An enormous white whale, a persistent musical motif, or a brilliant Mediterranean sun, are neutral phenomena as such, but the particular whale named Moby Dick, or Vinteuil's haunting strain in *Swann's Way*, or the sun's overpowering presence in Camus' *The Stranger* : these are metaphors capable of absorbing the forces active in the work, and of touching the reader with their overflowing energies.

Ezra Pound noted that a poetic image is "that which presents an intellectual and emotional complex in an instant of time, a unification of disparate ideas," and then, commenting on the powerful effect which such images can have on the reader: "It is the presentation of such a 'complex' instantaneously which gives us that sense of sudden liberation; that sense of freedom from time limits and space limits.[14] The philosopher Hans Meyerhoff expressed a similar thought when he wrote: "The recollection of the *madeleine* is the clue to the reconstruction of Proust's life, which means that the sum total of his life is potentially co-present (or simultaneous) with this single event."[15]

Some works may not contain a dominant image which could be said to stand at the aesthetic center of the text; there may be no shield of Achilles, no white whale, no taste of a madeleine and no Wasteland, to incarnate somehow the essence of the work. In such a case, the encompassing image may be an ever shifting Concrete Universal — not usually capable of being expressed in words — nourished by newly perceived constellations of successive events. This condition prevails, I believe, when one recalls to the mind's eye a play like *Macbeth*, or a novel like *War and Peace*. The image is subjective, in the sense that it will be different with each new experience of the work, but it is by no means arbitrary. An adequate image will be at one with the work's meaning in terms of one particular experience of it, and it will be completely present in an instant, no matter how long it would take to rehearse the succession of events which contribute to the instantaneous presentness of the fiction.

Pavanne and Divisions (New York: 1918), p. 96.
Time in Literature (Berkeley: 1960), p. 49. One wonders why Meyerhoff found it necessary to include the author's life in "this single event." The inclusion of extra-textual data seems difficult to justify.

Chapter Two

THE SEARCH FOR THE SUFFICIENT
MOMENT: TIME AND GEOMETRY

> . . . at the still point, there the dance is,
> . . .
>
> T.S. ELIOT, "BURNT NORTON"

> I will show you somthing infinite and indivisible. It is a
> point which moves everywhere with infinite speed; for it is
> everywhere and is wholly present in every place.
>
> Blaise Pascal, Pensée no. 231,
trans. A.J. Kreilsheimer

DISCOMFITURES

An awareness of seasonal changes, the nocturnal processions in the sky, and the confident expectation that the rhythms of nature will continue into the future — these are the conditions which made it possible,in an anthropological perspective, to establish norms for the measurement of time. At some stage of pre-history it became necessary to relate to one's environment in temporal as well as spatial terms. When the flow of events could be divided into successive segments, it became more accessible to the mind. Days, seasons and years occurred in rhythmic progression and became linguistic objectifications that reflected the modalities of perception. A single continuum of time, universally applicable, became the dominant historical perception in the western world; the simplicity of a steady temporal progression, its easy divisibility into past, present and future, long served to allay doubts and discomforts regarding the ultimate nature of time. Whenever time itself was invoked, as an abstract concept and as the source of its concrete temporal manifestations, it lost its ideational purity and became submerged in spatial metaphors, like astronomical conjunctions, or the angle formed by the hands on a clock. Somewhere behind the endless succession of events lay the mystery of time itself, the inviolate object of philosophic speculation and, for the faithful, the vehicle of its own transcendence. "As we are men," Paul Tillich remarked in one of his sermons, "we are aware of the eternal to which we belong and from which we are estranged by the bondage of time."[1]

One of the most striking juxtapositions of human and divine temporal modalities occurs in the Gospel of John where the Pharisees take Jesus to task for asserting that he had seen the living Abraham, when in fact it was obvious, as he stood before them on the Mount of Olives, that he was less than fifty years old. Jesus' reply shines through a syntactical error of the greatest consequence: ". . . Before Abraham was, I am" (John 8.58), words which violate logic and the sequence of tenses, and thereby make language, in a moment of highest poetry, a conduit to eternity. Jesus' words could be believed, but never understood.

Only when man is estranged from himself can he reflect upon his self. Innocence is an unreflective state, and its opposite makes knowledge and guilt appear synonymous. The emergence of history, like the child's growing awareness of the gradations of temporality, signals a trade-off between innocence and self-consciousness, and when the bargain is consummated, our pre-eminence in the world is rigidly circumscribed by "not-yets" and "no mores." Such have been the wages of Original Sin, or in secular language, the consequences of the first "disobedient" steps leading up the ladder of civilization. The exhilaration which accompanies intellectual advancement is undermined by a feeling of insecurity at the center of our being.

A most suggestive exploration of "innocence" is at the heart of Heinrich von Kleist's essay "On Marionettes" (*Über das Marionettentheater*), written in 1810, in which mechanically articulated puppets are pitted against living dancers and actors who self-consciously ply their trade.

Kleist's odd ruminations on what he playfully called "the jointed folk" (*Gliedermänner*) continue to attract attention because they add up to a startlingly vivid formulation of an ancient problem: the distinction between natural and contrived behavior, or between instinctual and conscious movements of the psyche. The essay is in the form of a conversation between Kleist, as the author-narrator, and a dancing teacher referred to as C., who is exceedingly fond of marionettes and believes that dancers and actors could learn much from them. C. argues along the following lines: the articulated figurines, manipulated by the puppeteers from the scaffolding above a miniature stage, have a center of

---

[1] *The Eternal Now* (New York, 1963), p. 123.

gravity which governs their posture and the quality of their movements. Some limbs are selected for separate control from above, while others follow, "like a pendulum," the dictates of gravity. Now dancers and actors — and by extension human beings in general — by virtue of being conscious of the effect of their movements and expressions, are out of touch with their center of gravity, and hence have lost their instinctual grace; they are reduced to contriving a kinesthetic equivalent of their feelings and adjusting it by a calculus of its probable effect on others.

C. expresses his dissatisfaction with certain contemporary performers and speaks of a Daphne who, in turning back to see a pursuing Apollo, twists her body as though she were about to break in two, and of a Paris who offers the apple to Venus with a most incongrous movement of his elbow. In summing up, C. declares:

> Such blunders are unavoidable . . . since we have eaten from the tree of knowledge. But the gates of paradise are barred and the angel drives us away; we must make the journey around the world and see if perchance we may slip in again through the back door.[2]

By way of confirming C.'s examples of the destructive effects of self-consciousness, Kleist, as the narrator, draws on an episode from his own memory, according to which a handsome youth of sixteen had emerged from a swim in a lake and, as was his habit, had seated himself on a stool, placed a foot on his knee, and proceeded to dry himself. It so happened that the young man had recently become acquainted with the classical sculpture known as *Spinario*, the "Thorn Puller," and that he was suddenly struck by the similarity of the famous work with his own posture. An impulse of vanity caused the youth to reach for a mirror in order to verify the resemblance. The incident marked the beginning of a profound change in him. During the ensuing days and weeks, the young man's movements began to lose their easy grace and became increasingly awkward. Girls who could usually be seen about him, began to stay away. His natural charm which, like a magnet, had drawn others into his vicinity, was irreparably lost. His self-consciousness had become a wall between himself and his "center of gravity." No longer innocent, he had entered into a self-conscious adulthood.

"Solche Mißgriffe . . . sind unvermeidlich, seitdem wir von dem Baum der Erkenntnis gegessen haben. Doch das Paradies ist verriegelt und der Cherub hinter uns; wir müssen die Reise um die Welt machen, und sehen, ob es vielleicht von hinten irgendwo wieder offen ist." (*Sämtliche Werke und Briefe*, ed. Helmut Sembdner (Munich, 1961), II, 342. Translation mine.

This image, permeated with classical allusions, including an echo of
Narcissus, is close enough to familiar legend — as well as to daily life —
to be readily accepted. On the other hand, the elaborate account of the
marionettes seems far less plausible. It is not easy to agree with the view
that the charm of the puppets lies in the gracefulness of their movements. A brief reflection will show such charm to have a different
source. The mechanical and typically jerky movements of the marionettes tend to formalize and stylize — more radically than human
actors or dancers would — the characters which they are meant to
embody. Thus the aesthetic distance which they create between themselves and the audience is oddly, and charmingly, contradicted by the
spectators' familiarity with their human models. The clearly noticeable
manipulation of the puppets from above supplies an emphatic "as if"
to the action and places special demands on the audience's imaginative
participation. The mechanical and always somewhat imperfect imitation
of organic life results in a playfulness of the proceedings on the stage
absent from traditional drama. Despite such objections, Kleist is successful in making his readers believe — at least provisionally — in the
marionettes' special gracefulness. Somehow the incongruity surrounding some of the illustrations does not obscure the point of the essay but
on the contrary, brings it into bold relief. The point, or thesis, finds its
most felicitous formulation in these remarks by the philosophical dancing teacher which conclude the short essay:

> Just as two lines which cross [said C.], and which after their passage
> through infinity suddenly appear again on the other side of their intersection
> . . . so too, when knowledge has so to speak passed through infinity, will
> grace be restored; so that it will appear in its purest form either in a body
> entirely devoid of consciousness, or else in one that possesses it to an infinite
> degree, i.e., in a marionette, or in a god.
>
> Do you mean, I said somewhat distractedly, that we should eat once more
> from the Tree of Knowledge in order to fall back into the state of innocence?
>
> I do indeed, answered C.; that is the last chapter of the history of the
> world.[3]

By making use of a simple geometric principle, Kleist has translated
the religious meaning of the Fall into a kind of poetic anthropology.

---

[3] "Doch so, wie sich der Durchschnitt zweier Linien, auf der einen Seite eines
Punktes, nach dem Durchgang durch das Unendliche, plötzlich wieder auf der
andern Seite einfindet . . . : so findet sich auch, wenn die Erkenntnis gleichsam
durch ein Unendliches gegangen ist, die Grazie wieder ein. . . .
Mithin, sagte ich ein wenig zerstreut, müßen wir wieder von dem Baum der
Erkenntnis essen, und in den Stand der Unschuld zurückzufallen?
Allerdings, antwortete er; das ist das letzte Kapitel von der Geschichte der Welt.
(*Ibid.*, II, 345.)

since we have lost the Eden of our infancy — as individuals and as a race — we dream persistently of returning to it, and if we follow the poet's playful metaphysics, we may indeed think "somewhat distractedly" (*ein wenig zerstreut*) of reentering paradise "through the back door," once the fruits from the Tree of Knowledge have become our exclusive diet.

A geometric point of dimensionless infinity must be traversed if one wishes to attain to the innocence of absolute knowledge. Intellectual and religious history is replete with such verbal somersaults and paradoxical designs intended to convey a rationally inaccessible, mystical transcendency.

Because of the importance to our discussion of "the point," where a limitless expanse coincides with the infinitely small, and where eternity is congruent with the infinitesimal moment, we will survey the major phases of its evolution. Since its appearance in the Christian era — in its characteristically paradoxical form — its function has been shared by the diverse areas of mathematical abstraction, religious mysticism, and poetic symbolism. Its remarkable persistence in the mainstream of Western thought will go a long way toward explaining its continuing, though more covert, presence in modern literature. Of course, by no means all polar oppositions should be regarded as variants of the same basic image, nor should they all be seen as answering the same basic needs. After all, the rhetorical device of paradox has a fascination of its own, and the various ways in which verbal and semantic oppositions are reconciled produce satisfactions which are perhaps best explained by a psychological theory of the kind offered by I.A. Richards in his *Principles of Literary Criticism* (1925) in which the power to bring about an equipoise of many disparate impulses is seen as the essential quality of literary art. The tension which keeps successiveness and simultaneity in a state of inimical rapport, as well as the efforts to fuse concreteness and abstraction, experience and meaning, into a unified whole — these are discernible in numerous human activities. For example, the desire for ever increasing speed with which an individual may be conveyed from place to place has as its limit the idea of infinite speed, and hence omnipresence in an all-encompassing still point. Or the legendary quest for the elixir of youth which, if sufficiently potent, might provide a substitute for life eternal. The immaturity of such longings becomes apparent in the light of Paul Tillich's terse comment: ". . . there is no time *after* time, but there is eternity *above* time."[4] An extended youthfulness would be like a child's rendering of the eternal now. And in the matter of movement from one location to another, the greatest imaginable

---

Paul Tillich, *op. cit.*, p. 125.

velocity is placed in rapport with the smallest; an intimation of infinite speed merges with an intimation of total rest. There is a coming-full-circle, analogous to the Kleistian "journey around the world," and at the end of it, the metaphysical click that signals the transit into an ever-present tense. When movement, or successiveness, seeks to be synonymous with stillness, or simultaneity, we also approach the paradoxical essence of literature so memorably evoked in the "still point" in T.S. Eliot's "Burnt Norton": ". . . neither flesh nor fleshless;/Neither from nor towards; at the still point, there the dance is."

FROM PLOTINUS TO PASCAL

The geometric point, as well as the circle, have long served as symbols of infinity, though to conceive the point as a non-dimensional *locus* at the intersection of lines required a high degree of abstraction. It attained its special significance only with the advent of Euclidian geometry in the third century B.C.

Plotinus, some five hundred years after Euclid, combined the endlessness of the periphery with the non-dimensionality of the center in order to create a symbol of an all-encompassing and all-pervasive unity, and passed on to the theologians and mystics an emblematic design which was carried forward through the Middle Ages and the Renaissance to its provisional *finale* in the seventeenth century with Kepler, Pascal and Newton. While the interpretation of its meaning underwent numerous changes, its simple structure remained essentially intact throughout its protracted presence in the European consciousness; in spite of several interpretive permutations, its capacity to figure infinity, or eternity, remained unimpaired. Plotinus describes the image as follows:

> There is, we may put it, something that is center; about it a circle of light shed from it; round center and first circle alike, another circle, light from light; outside that again, not another circle of light but one which lacking light of its own, must borrow. (*Enneads*, IV, 3, 17)[5]

The center of the circle or sphere (the two figures are used interchangeably), residing at the confluence of radii, signals an absolute unity, regardless of the observer's vantage point: seen from without, the center appears as an infinitely contracted sphere; from within, as a point at the moment of expansion, or as an "unextended extension" (*Enn.* VI

---

[5] *Plotinus on the Nature of the Soul*, trans. Stephen McKenna. (London and Boston 1924), III, 28. Subsequent citations are from this edition.

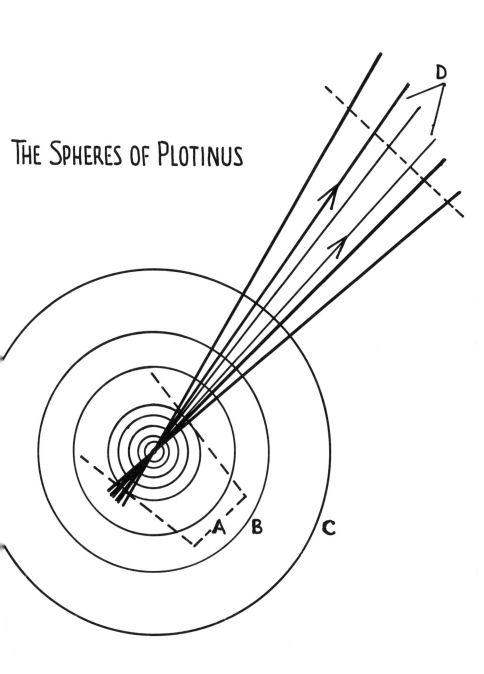

THE SPHERES OF PLOTINUS

8, 18). Here is the infinitely concentrated, intelligible reality which Plotinus liked to call the World Sun, in accordance with a by then well-established Pythagorean tradition. It is conceived as holding within itself an infinite number of radii which constitute the innermost, infinitely small, sphere. Indeed the concentric spheres, expanding from the center, are at first still so closely related to the "point," that their circumference is infinitely small and cannot yet be segmented by the radii.

While the innermost spheres (A) are seen as unmoving and indistinguishable from the center, the middle and outer ones (B, C) are revolving and divided into discrete segments by the transversing radii. If the mind moves from the periphery toward the center, then the radii become symbols of the yearning for the One, the ultimate divine unity; but if the mind embarks on a centrifugal course, the radii symbolize the road to the world of appearances located in the outermost sphere which is broken up into segments. While Plotinus makes clear that sensible objects owe their being to the One, the transition from the center to the periphery is difficult, because the phenomenal world must manifest itself in space and time. The innermost spheres, on the other hand, which are infinitely close to being a non-dimensional central point, cannot be spatially or temporally segmented (see ill.)

Individual human souls are microcosmic analogies of the Absolute One. Both are indivisible.

> . . . the soul, essentially a unity, becomes adequate to omnipresence; its unity sets it outside of quantitative measurement, the characteristic of that order which has but a counterfeit unity, an appearance of participation.
> (*Enn.* VI, 5, 9)

Eight centuries before Plotinus, Parmenides had also envisioned the sphere and its center as a figure for the universe, but in his case it was an undifferentiated homogeneous bulk[6] whose outer surface corresponded to the limits of the universe. Plotinus, however, while acknowledging his debt to Parmenides, derived his teaching concerning the One, not from the pre-Socratic philosopher, but from Plato. The sphere of Parmenides was a miniature version, an actual model, of the universe, made up of an undifferentiated, primal substance, while Plotinus was explicit in referring to his version as an intelligible, non-material sphere and in proposing it only as an illustrative likeness. Unlike the sphere of Parmenides, that of Plotinus symbolized a hierarchical structure of being, ruled and pervaded by an unchanging Absolute.

---

[6] H. Diels and W. Kranz, *Die Fragmente der Vorsokratiker*, 7th ed. (Berlin, 1954), I, 239.

The significance of placing the Absolute in the center of Being can hardly be overestimated. It is a step which laid the philosophic groundwork for an aspect of developing Christian theology which sought ways in which Divine Infinity or Eternity could be conceived as ruling over all aspects of the finite world. Plotinus had vigorously upheld the division between the imperfect material world of the senses and the spiritual realm of the Unconditional. In so doing he adhered to the bifocal Platonic mode of vision, which proved to be so suitable for absorption into Christian dogma. The objects of the senses were merely transitory manifestations of their "real" and stable paradigms from which they derived, but with which they must not be confused.

Some Roman philosophers, and above all the Doctors of the Church, adopted the neo-Platonic image and reinterpreted its geometry in Christian terms. In the sixth century, Boethius developed a particularly rich formulation. Those of St. Bonaventure and Thomas Aquinas in the thirteenth century are quite similar, though shorter and in closer adherence to the circle-center formula:

Boethius: If one says that eternity signifies a measureless existence, one must reply that one does not thereby exhaust the meaning of the word 'eternity'; because this means not only interminability, but also simultaneousness; and if, on the other hand, by the mode of interminability one must understand an intelligible circumference, without beginning and without end, on the other hand by reason of its simultaneousness one must understand simplicity and indivisibility as modes of the center; and these two things are affirmed concerning the Divine Being at one and the same time, because He is at once simple and infinite; and so it is that one must understand the circularity as eternity.[7]

St. Bonaventure: Because [the Divinity] is eternal and absolutely present, It surrounds and enters all durations, existing, as it were, both as a center and as a circumference. Because It is absolutely uniform and all-encompassing, It exists within all things and without all things, and for this reason the center of the intelligible sphere is everywhere and the circumference nowhere.[8]

Thomas Aquinas: Eternity resembles the center of the circle; even though simple and indivisible, it yet comprehends the whole course of time, and every part of it is equally present.[9]

It was only in the later Middle Ages — in the context of the Plotinian concentric spheres — an interpenetration of the hitherto separate realms was brought about, and this was done by replacing the attribute

---

Quaestiones Disputatae De Mysterio Trinitatis, ed. Quaracchi. 9.5, art. 1, 7-8, *Opera Omnia*.
Itinerarium Mentis ad Deum, cap. v, 8.
Declaratio quorundorum articulorum, op. 2.

"intelligible" with "infinite." It fell to the anonymous authors of a tract called *Liber XXIV philosophorum* to initiate this mingling of the palpable world with transcendent forms and ideas.

In commenting on the writings of the German mystic Meister Eckhart (c. 1260-1327), Heinrich Denifle in 1886 became the first scholar to bring this little book to the attention of a learned, theologically oriented circle of scholars. He noted that Eckhart had repeatedly referred to the book in order to find support for his own views.[10] Yet Denifle did not recognize the significance of the anonymous tract. He saw neither its decisive influence on Meister Eckhart's thought, nor its role, albeit indirect, in the unfolding of the geometrics of Renaissance mysticism. Instead Denifle came to the conclusion that the *Book of Twenty-Four Philosophers* was a "meaningless piece" of derivative religious speculation.

In 1913, Clemens Baeumker published a scholarly edition of the *Liber*, along with an analysis of Denifle's negative evaluation, and while emphasizing the book's neo-Platonic roots, carefully singled out those passages which were at variance with Plotinus' spherical imagery.[11] It was Baeumker's meticulous and creative scholarship which provided the basis for Dietrich Mahnke's work on the "infinite sphere and all-encompassing center."[12]

The medieval tract contains twenty-four propositions dealing with aspects of the existence of God. It begins and ends with a reference to Hermes Trismegistus[13] and thereby aligns itself with the neo-Pythagorean "hermetic" tradition which according to various mostly unreliable sources, had its beginnings with the *Asclepius*, a book long falsely attributed to the Roman satirist Apuleius who lived in the second century A.D.[14] This is a work of unknown authorship — possibly produced as late as the fourth century — written in the form of a dialogue between Hermes Trismegistus and his disciple Asclepius. Lengthy passages dealing with the cosmic significance of numbers alternate with discussions

---

[10] See Heinrich Denifle and Ehrle, *Archiv für die Literatur- und Kirchengeschichte des Mittelalters*, II (1886), pp. 427, 429, *et passim*.

[11] "Das pseudo-hermetische 'Buch der vierundzwanzig Meister' (Liber XXIV philosophorum)" in *Studien und Charakteristiken zur Geschichte der Philosophie, insbesondere des Mittelalters* (Münster, 1927), pp. 194-214.

[12] *Unendliche Sphäre und Allmittelpunkt*, in Deutsche Vierteljahrsschrift, Buchreihe 23 (Halle, Saale, 1937). The results of Mahnke's scholarship provided the conceptual basis for this chapter.

[13] "Incipit liber de propositionibus sive de regulis theologiae, qui dicitur Termegisti Philosophi." — "Explicit liber Termegisti de regulis theologiae cum commento Chalcidii, ut puto." (First and last sentence of the *Liber*, as published by Baeumker, *op. cit.*).

[14] See Walter Scott, *Hermetica* (Oxford, 1924), pp. 79-81.

of quasi-religious mysteries. Hellenistic and pseudo-Egyptian oracular pronouncements combine to form an amalgam perculiar to this work. Hermes, or Mercurius Trismegistus, is seen as a god-like figure, a sort of reincarnation of the Egyptian god Tehuti, or Thot. In any case, Hermes Trismegistus came to stand for "hermetic" wisdom and was cited as an oracular authority to which subsequent religious thinkers such as St. Augustine and mystics would frequently refer. The fourteenth-century English theologian and mathematician Thomas Bradwardine, citing St. Augustine as his source, could speak of Hermes Trismegistus as "clarus propheta et philosophus gloriosus."[15]

In addition to its hermetic components, *The Book of Twenty-Four Philosophers*, which Mahnke tentatively assigns to the late twelfth century, contained neo-Platonic and, to a lesser extent, Aristotelian elements. We will cite only those four of its twenty-four propositions which are relevant to our study:

1. God is a monad which engenders a monad and which reflects in itself its own ardor.
2. God is an infinite sphere whose center is everywhere and whose circumference nowhere.
3. God is whole in every part of himself.
18. God is a sphere which contains as many circumferences as points.[16]

Each of the twenty-four propositions is enlarged upon and elucidated by its anonymous authors. Our main concern is with number 2, but because of its special relevance to our study, we will cite the *explication* appended to proposition 18 as well:

to No. 2: This definition is offered by way of representing the first cause as a living center. For the scope of its extension is above and beyond any limit. Therefore, wherever the center is found, it has no dimension. The soul seeking the circumference of the circle will be transported to the infinite, because whatever is created without dimension is without beginning. Thus there are no limits.

to No. 18: This follows from the second proposition, because inasmuch as the sphere is entirely without dimension —which is to say, of infinite dimension — it will have no outer

---

[15] Baeumker, *op. cit.*, p. 199.
[16] 1. "Deus est monas, monadem gigens, in se suum reflectens ardorem."
2. "Deus est sphaera infinita, cuius centrum est ubique, circumferentia nusquam."
3. "Deus est totus in quolibet sui."
18: "Deus est sphaera, cuius tot sunt circumferentiae, quot sunt puncta."

limit whatever. Hence there is no point which could be located outside the circle's circumference.[17]

The eighteenth proposition is an elaboration of the second and emphasizes the interchangeability of the circumference with the center, so that the "point" can be seen to hold within itself the maximum in its absolute concentration, a notion reflected in one of Eckhart's professions of mystical faith: "In divine things, everything is in everything else and the maximum is in the minimum."[18] The way was now clear for much of the subsequent circular imagery which was intended to symbolize the fusion, not only of the spiritual with the phenomenal world, but also of the double spatial infinities of vastness and smallness, and henceforth the preferred descriptive term for the circle tended to be "infinite" rather than "intellectual" or "intelligible," as it had been in Plotinus, St. Augustine and Boethius. It is possible to show how the transition occurred by tracing it in the works of Meister Eckhart. Near the turn of the thirteenth century, he still spoke of the Plotinian "intelligible" sphere, but in later writings he began to use "infinite" as an additional attribution. Nor did he neglect to indicate the source: "God . . . is an intellectual, infinite sphere *(sphaera intellectualis infinita)* whose center is everywhere and whose circumference nowhere . . . as is written *in that book.*"[19]

But at the onset of a more man-centered outlook of the early Renaissance, it was the theologian-philosopher Nicolas de Cusa (1401-1464) who carried forward the geometric tradition and became its most influential proponent. Strongly indebted to Meister Eckhart, a German like himself, Cusanus — as the cardinal was known to many — made the sphere and its attributes the keystone of his main work *Of Ignorant Wisdom (De docta ignorantia)* because it served him as the most adequate symbol for his life-long quest: the reconciliation between sense experience and the transcendent Absolute. Elements of Christianized neo-Platonism and Thomistic scholasticism were important components of his theodicy. But his overriding adherence, as Ernst Cassirer convincingly showed, was to Plato.[20] Like Plato, Cusanus saw the world irreparably divided between the conditional and the absolute. There was no possibility of attaining to the "maximum" by progressing in stages from the known to the unknown:

[17] Propositions and *explicationes* cited from Baeumker, *Das Pseudo-hermetische Buch*, pp. 208, 212. Translation mine.
[18] Denifle and Ehrle, *Archiv*, II, 571. Translation mine.
[19] Denifle and Ehrle, *Archiv*, II, 571. My underline.
[20] *The Individual and the Cosmos in Renaissance Philosophy*, trans. Mario Donati (New York, 1963). (First published in German in 1926.)

From the self-evident fact that there is no gradation from infinite to finite, it is clear that the simple maximum is not to be found where we meet degrees of more or less.[21]

But because the infinite was for him the goal of all learning, any quest for it entailed the hard-won recognition of man's essential ignorance. The maximum could be described only in terms of what it is *not*:

A finite intellect, therefore, cannot by means of comparison reach the absolute truth of things. . . . The relationship of our intellect to the truth is like that of a polygon to the circle; the resemblance to the circle grows with the multiplication of the angles of the polygon; . . . it is clear, therefore, that all we know of the truth is that the absolute truth is beyond our reach. The truth which can be neither more nor less than it is, is the most absolute necessity, while in contrast with it, our intellect is possibility.[22]

Yet despite the cleavage between the relative and the absolute, Cusanus envisioned a rapport between the two. It was to be brought about by symbolic participation, a method which he developed and advocated in the treatise *De Coniecturis*. True learning, according to his reasoning, can have both positive and negative consequences. While it must lead us to a recognition of our permanent incapacity to know the truth, the same learning can also enable us to achieve a *symbolic* apprehension of truth. And of all symbols, that of the sphere, or circle, was for Cusanus the most conducive to an awareness of the Maximum, in which all polar oppositions are fused into a perfect unity. Immediately preceding the praise of the circle in his *De docta ignorantia*, Cusanus employed the following formulation for the idea of the deity: "In Him, in fact, the beginning is such that the beginning and the end are one." Then, in the next paragraph, there follows a description of the symbol by means of which we might participate in Him:

All this we gather from the infinite circle, which having neither beginning nor end is eternal, is infinitely one and infinite in capacity. Now, because this circle is infinite, its diameter is also infinite; and the diameter is the circumference, for this circle is infinitely one and there cannot be more than one infinite. But the middle of an infinite diameter is infinite, and, as the middle is the center, diameter and circumference are one and the same. The lesson which we here learn in our ignorance is that the Maximum, which is at once the minimum, is incomprehensible; and in it the center is the circumference.[23]

Because the circle is the "absolutely ultimate perfection of figures" (*ultima perfectio figurarum qua maior non est*), it is necessary, according

[21] Nicolas Cusanus, *Of Learned Ignorance*, trans. Germain Heron (New Haven, 1954), I, 3, p. 11.

[22] *Op. cit.*, pp. 11-12.

[23] *Op. cit.*, I, 21, p. 47.

to Cusanus, in view of man's fundamental ignorance, to rise above the
limitations of our finite capacities and to extend the geometric image
into an infinite number of "corresponding figures," so that a multiplicity of necessarily imperfect representations may help to evoke and symbolize the simple idea of the infinite which "cannot be represented by
any figure."[24]

Nicolas de Cusa was among the first to move resolutely from religious
mysticism to a mathematically grounded exploration of the cosmos.
While the infinite sphere was for him a symbol which allows us to participate in divine perfection, it was also to be regarded as the most adequate representation of the physical universe (the sphere was now no
longer "intelligible" or "intellectual," but emphatically "infinite").
Hence he spoke as both astronomer and theologian when he held that
there is "a world machine whose center, so to speak, is everywhere,
whose circumference is nowhere; for God is its circumference and center
and He is everywhere and nowhere."[25] In astronomical terms, this
meant that the earth could not be the true center of the universe, even
in the geocentric cosmos of de Cusa's time, because none of the planetary spheres, being involved in matter, could be true circles. However, in a metaphysical and mystical view, it meant that the earth was
indeed a true center, as was every other point in the infinite universe.

The conception of the ubiquitous center enables Cusanus to apply
geometric symbols to the human soul as well, for rather than being a
faded representation of a divine essence, it could now be seen as an
infinitely small point encompassing the Maximum. However, for each
individual the transition to infinity had to be preceded by the hard intellectual labor leading to the highest level of "learned ignorance." The
first step of the quest required the full panoply of reason, particularly
as it applies to mathematics and geometry. The second major step consisted of a critique of reason leading to a full awareness of its limitations.
In this way, the recognition of the symbolic power inherent in geometric
figures, preeminently in the circle and sphere, could become the highest
boon to the human condition, for such recognition would make it possible for learnedly ignorant individuals to participate in the Absolute.
Cusanus never doubted that the soul of man is the "center" which by
virtue of its share in divine ubiquity, seeks to break out of its confining
human compass and to affirm its rapport with the Absolute. The stance
of the prototypal Renaissance artistic personality, supremely confident
of being an instrument of divine creation, was therefore, to a considerable degree, laid by the *quattrocento* mathematical and mystical genius
of de Cusa.

---

[24] *Op. cit.*, I, 12, p. 27.
[25] *Op. cit.*, I, 12, p. 27.

But why should the human "center" differ so markedly from other points in the universe since, according to the well-known formula, "the center is everywhere?" The answer lies in man's position in the cosmic hierarchy. Cusanus accepted a good part of his medieval heritage, in particular the scholastic dogma of man's preeminent position "a little lower than the angels." He taught that man was peculiarly suited — in contrast to other creatures — to unite with the Maximum, so that each separate soul may symbolize the essence of humanity as a whole and that the race of man may be "assumed into the most intimate possible union with God."[26]

De Cusa's teachings concerning the centrality of man can be transposed, without great difficulty, into a modern context: man's psychic center appears differentiated from other points in the universe to the extent that it possesses the attribute of consciousness. It is simultaneously subject and object. While the subjective "I" creates itself, its structure typically also becomes the object of contemplation which in turn can be observed by another self-reflecting "I," so that an infinite series of mirror reflections will appear to those who embark on such an inward journey. It is such self-consciousness which makes modern man pre-eminent and which, most uncomfortably, makes him a "center."

The image of the circle had undergone an important change. With de Cusa it had become irreversibly "infinite" rather than a purely spiritual and abstract conception, and as a result the phenomenal world was no longer pushed outward toward the periphery. In the concentric and "intelligible" spheres of Plotinus, the divine essence was located at the center and its emanations had moved outward along the radii toward the outermost sphere, which represented the transient world of man's concrete environment.[27] When the attribute "infinite" first began to replace the earlier term in Meister Eckhart's writings, it was not possible to foresee that the new designation would in fact fit the surrounding physical universe, where infinity is most readily associated with a spherical firmament, with the earth at the center. In de Cusa's symbolic representation, the radii could be plausibly represented as pointing centripetally, from the infinity of the outer circumference towards a central point, rather than centrifugally, from the Absolute One toward a segmented periphery, as in Plotinus. (See next page.)

Having said this, it becomes necessary to retract, at least in part, the notion of a turnabout in the circular image because, after all, in both Plotinus and de Cusa, the direction of the flow of divine energy must be understood metaphorically, imagined rather than grasped by the

---

[26] See fn. 23 above.
[27] *Op. cit.*, III, 3, p. 137.

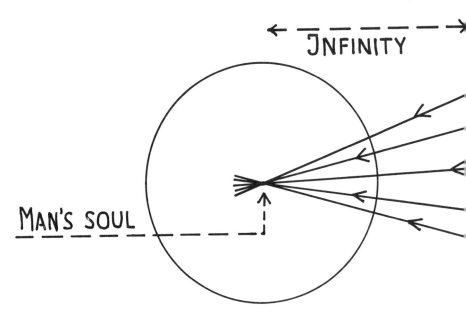

mind attempting to orient itself in the unfathomable context of infinity. For Cusanus, mathematical signs and geometric forms not only *represented* the visible and tangible world, but were themselves part of a reality which allowed "learnedly ignorant" individuals to participate in the Absolute. And so, while the logical consequence of de Cusa's use of "infinity" would appear to be a reversal of the flow of divine energy, it would be more in keeping with the spirit of Renaissance mysticism to assume such a flow to be multi-, or rather, omni-directional. The spirit and practice of mathematical mysticism nourished all subsequent cosmological constructs of the Renaissance, and it is only in comparatively recent times that astronomy assumed a posture of a discipline sufficient unto itself, independent of theology and, as far as possible, of philosophy as well.

The Italian scholar Marsilio Ficino (1433-1499) who lived a generation after de Cusa, did much to bring a Christianized version of Neo-Platonism into the mainstream of European thought. The insights derived from his translations of Plato and Plotinus from Greek into Latin, as well as the mystical notions gleaned from his edition of the *Asclepius*, were incorporated in his influential writings on Christian theology, particularly his *Theologia Platonica*. Like Cusanus before him, Ficino adopted the image of the circle, though it was Plotinus' version of it which dominated his commentaries. His circle remained "intelligible" and hence did not impinge on physical reality. Accordingly the

"ubiquitous center" was entirely of the spirit and excluded any participation by the senses.[28]
Most prominently, it was Giordano Bruno (1548-1600) who carried forward the geometric tradition of de Cusa. The philosophic dialogues which make up the volume on *The Cause, the Origin and the One (De la causa, principio e uno)* show Bruno freely conceding his indebtedness to the revered master, not only with respect to general notions such as the reconciliation of opposites in the realm of the infinite, but also when dealing with as specific a subject as the symbolic significance of the infinite circle:

> . . . take notice of the signs and verifications, by means of which we wish to conclude that the contraries coincide in one; . . . you shall take the signs from mathematics, and the verifications from the other moral and speculative faculties. Hence, as regards the signs, tell me: What thing is more contrary to the straight line than the circle? What thing is more contrary to the straight line than the curve? Yet they coincide in the principal and in the smallest part; since, as Cusanus, the discoverer of the most beautiful secrets of geometry, has divinely observed — what difference will you find between the smallest arc and the smallest cord? Further, in the greatest; what difference will you find between the infinite circle and the straight line?[29]

Bruno took the most radical consequence of the circle-center imagery when he noted that the ultimate constituent parts of physical nature are centers, or points, which are infinite in the same way as the circle is infinite. These ultimate, indivisible centers are everywhere, and Bruno knew how to characterize them succinctly by laying open the root of a key word and making it visible to the reader:

> Hence, the in-dividual is not different from the "dividual," the simplest entity [not different] from the infinite, the center [not different from] the circumference.[30]

While de Cusa had been above all concerned with the role of the individual soul and with its rapport to the Maximum, Bruno placed greater emphasis on the physical world, without thereby in the least denying the insights of his admired model. Bruno's speculative bent led him to

---

[28] For a detailed treatment of Ficino's use of the circular image, see Dietrich Mahnke, (fn. 12 above), pp. 60-66.
[29] Cited from Sidney Greenberg, *The Infinite in Giordano Bruno* (New York, 1950), p. 169.
[30] "Dunque, l'individuo non è differente dal dividuo, il simplicissimo da l'infinito, il centro da la circonferenza." Ed. Romano Amerio, *Opere di Giordano Bruno e di Tommaso Campannella* (Milano, 1956), p. 401. Translation mine.

dwell at some length on the physical equivalence, in the realm of infinity, between the center and the circumference. For the voyage to infinity, one could therefore set one's course in an outward direction through the immensity of space, or else — with equal validity — travel centripetally toward the dimensionless center, or "monad." Thus, by availing himself of a term that had once been used in the *Book of Twenty-Four Philosophers* (in the first proposition), Bruno foreshadowed by a century its most famous elaboration in the monadology of Leibniz.

We can see the extent to which physical nature has now come to dominate the interpretation of an image which had once stood exclusively for the intellect, or the spirit, in a sentence like the following: "The actual figuration of the minimum in the plane is the circle, and in space, the sphere. Hence all physical atoms have a spherical shape . . . since every work of nature is necessarily a spherical unfolding of a unified center."[31] Bruno's work contains many philosophical hurdles and unresolved contradiction, as L. Olschki's lucid exposition shows,[32] but this need not trouble us, since our brief survey does not necessitate an evaluation of Bruno's philosophy. We are concerned with the stages of the circle-center image, and hence with Bruno's developing preoccupation with spatial and temporal infinity and with his forcefully stated conviction that each atom, or monad, is permeated by it:

> If the point does not differ from the body, the center from the circumference, the finite from the infinite, the maximum from the minimum, surely we can affirm that the universe is all center, or that the center of the universe is everywhere. . . .[33]

During his eight years of incarceration, Bruno became increasingly obdurate in his views, and while denying any heretical intention, he remained uncompromising in his conviction that natural science and philosophy, even when unaided by Christian dogma, could reveal ultimate truth.[34] He was among the early defenders of the Copernican heliocentric theory. His free-ranging geometric speculations led him beyond the reaches of reason to a personal faith in pantheism, which additionally contributed to his condemnation by the Inquisition and to death at the stake on the Campo di Fiori in Rome.

When, in the seventeenth century, Blaise Pascal applied his mathematical genius to the circular image of infinity, the confidence in man's

---

[31] Cited from Mahnke, *op. cit.*, p. 57.
[32] "Giordano Bruno," in *Deutsche Vierteljahrsschrift für Literaturwissenschaft und Geistesgeschichte*, II (1924), p. 77.
[33] Quoted from Greenberg, *op. cit.*, p. 162.
[34] See Giovanni Gentile, *Il pensiero del rinascimento* (Florence, 1940), pp. 259-310.

centrality had faded, and the hitherto unquestioned rapport between his soul and the infinite was lost. The image that had for so long stood for a comforting relationship between the mundane and the divine had now become a geometry of emptiness. The periphery was no longer symbolically accessible, and the ubiquitous spatial and temporal center lay hopelessly on the far side of the abyss which had opened between a conscious self and its innermost core. Once the pre-eminent and divinely inspired center, man was now at best able to recognize the wretchedness of his condition. A section of Pascal's *Pensée* on the "disproportion of man" reads as follows:

> For in the end, what is man's place in nature? Nothing compared to the infinite; all, compared to nothingness, a middle point between all and nothing.[35]

Even the mite (*le ciron*) which served Pascal as an example of the smallest possible creature, stands at the brink of an inward chasm of the infinitely small, while human beings would be representative of immensity from a mite's perspective. Neither the minimum nor the maximum was within man's reach, in Pascal's despairing view. Gone was de Cusa's optimism which grew out of a conviction of man's centrality within the divine sphere. In an earlier passage of the same *pensée*, Pascal observed:

> . . . we only give birth to atoms, at the expense of the reality of things. Nature is a sphere whose center is everywhere and whose circumference is nowhere. This is after all the greatest perceptible characteristic of God's omnipotence, that our imagination must lose itself in this thought.[36]

The individual is suspended in the mist of a terrifying and infinite emptiness, ignorant of where — at an abysmal depth within him — lies the indivisible and all-encompassing unity. Nor does he know why he was assigned a particular moment between past and future eternities. "I see only infinities on all sides which engulf me like an atom and like a shadow which lasts but an instant without return."[37] The disproportion of man is irremediable, for even if it were possible to take up position

---

5 "Car enfin qu'est-ce que l'homme dans la nature? Un néant à l'égard de l'infini, un tout à l'égard du néant, un milieu entre rien et tout." Ed. M. Léon Brunschvicg, *Pensées et opuscules* (Paris, 1952), *Pensée* no. 72. Translation mine.
5 ". . . nous n'enfantons que des atomes, au prix de la réalité des choses. C'est une sphère dont le centre est partout, la circonférence nulle part. Enfin c'est le plus grand caractère sensible de la toute puissance de Dieu, que notre imagination se perde dans cette pensée." *Ibid.*
7 *Pensée* no. 194.

at the center — in itself a futile endeavor — even then the circumference would fade into nowhere. And conversely, a view from the finite region where we dwell, reveals only a terrifying void (*ces espaces effroyables*)[38] which defeats all hope. "The infinite is annihilated in the presence of the infinite and becomes pure nothingness."[39]

This is a condition which, according to Pascal, will be acknowledged by all who are endowed with a penetrating and agile intellect and who, moreover, have highly intuitive perception arising from the "heart." Those who scorn the rhetoric of morality will show themselves to be true moralists, and the true philosophers are those who transcend the schemata of philosophy.[40]

But no matter how far the *esprit de finesse* takes such gifted individuals, its operation only serves to increase their wretchedness, because even the *esprit* must arise from an inevitable optical illusion since it is impossible for man to occupy more than a single vantage point at any moment. Pascal creates the image of a firebrand being whirled in a circle: the faster it moves, the more persuasively will it seem to approach the stable outline of a circumference.[41] But since the firebrand — or point of light — can actually be only at one place at any moment, it cannot be "everywhere" along the periphery.

In the realm of infinity, on the other hand, the point can be present simultaneously along the periphery and at the center; it can, in other words, encompass the antinomies of movement and rest. Hence the gulf between human limits and the divine absolute can never be bridged.

> I will show you something infinite and indivisible. It is a point which moves everywhere with infinite speed; for it is everywhere and is wholly present in every place.[42]

For Nicolas de Cusa, the "learned ignorance" had been a stepping stone for a symbolic participation in the Maximum. Moreover, man himself at his creative best, was identical with the center. For Pascal the more "learned" the ignorance, the greater man's impotence and despair. Surrounded by infinite emptiness he could not hope, through his own strength, to find any solid ground on which to stand, and therefore had nothing to lose, and everything to gain, by wagering on the existence of a Christian God.[43]

---

[38] *Ibid.*

[39] *Pensée* no. 233.

[40] See *Pensée* no. 4.

[41] *Pensée* no. 353.

[42] "Je vous veux donc faire voir une chose infinie et indivisible. C'est un point mouvant partout d'une vitesse infinie; car il est un en tous lieux et est tout entier en chaque endroit." *Pensée* no. 231.

[43] See *Pensée* no. 233.

Such are some of the geometric-mystical journeys on which, in the Christian era of Western intellectual history, many eminent thinkers had embarked. In all instances since Plotinus, there was a tendency to abrogate the distinction between the circumference and the center, because what was at stake was precisely the transcendence of their opposition and the ultimate equivalence of the two in infinity. The innermost circles of Plotinus signaled that the smallest of them would also be the closest to the "One," and would point to a perfection that can manifest itself equally in terms of either an expanded point or an infinitely contracted sphere.

But it is always the dimensionless point which is the object — the holy grail, as it were — from Plotinus to Pascal, without exception. It is the place of encompassing unity, the crucible in which ultimate oppositions are fused. Plotinus, Cusanus, Giordano Bruno and Pascal all mastered, and sometimes advanced, the level of mathematical and geometrical knowledge, and their writings are testimony to an encompassing sensibility within which — in sharp contrast to the twentieth century — the mathematical and mystical imagination were compatible and even largely congruent.

The tradition of numerological and geometric mysticism came to an end with Kepler, Pascal and Newton. Henceforth the exact sciences became more compartmentalized, while metaphysics and theology grew timid and self-consciously metaphorical in their use of terms borrowed from the sciences. The image of the infinite circle with its ubiquitous center presented no exception to this tendency. The center in particular, most frequently envisioned simply as a point without dimension, had long fired the imagination of poets and now became their possession. While such a center, or point, encompassed infinity in both the spatial and temporal sense, it was the intractably problematic nature of time rather than space for which it most often became the symbolic vehicle. It flourished as a *topos* and also as an imperious, though hidden, structural ideal for a luminous procession of poets like Goethe, Marcel Proust, Joyce, Virginia Woolf and Thomas Mann.

Chapter Three

DANTE'S VISIONARY JOURNEY TO THE ETERNAL MOMENT

> One point alone for me makes greater oblivion
> than five and twenty centuries upon the enterprise
> which made Neptune gaze upon the Argo's shadow.
>
> DANTE, *PARADISO* XXXIII

In the context of medieval religious writings one can observe how hermetic and neo-Platonic representations of eternity began to enter the Christian imagination and to enrich the repertoire of poetic diction. Since Dante's *Divina Commedia*, composed at the onset of the fourteenth century, became the most representative non-canonical work which yet embodied and exemplified orthodox Christian teaching, it will serve us well in our exploration of the manner in which an ancient heritage entered and informed high poetry. The great secular writers, figures like Goethe and contemporary authors like Thomas Mann, Virginia Woolf, T.S. Eliot and Samuel Beckett, employed mundane and close-at-hand equivalents of the old emblematic patterns, so that the hermetic motifs maintain no more than a residual presence now and can no longer be easily recognized as such. We will remember how in the metaphysical geometry of Plotinus the center symbolized The One, and note that the Doctors of the Church — St. Augustine and St. Thomas among them — carried forward such a concept of centrality into Christian dogma. In all cases, the center of the intelligible sphere, or circle, was the locus of non-dimensionality where space is annulled and all events occur both eternally and simultaneously. We will attempt to show here how a religious and mystical belief in an ultimate and all-encompassing unity became of primary concern to biblical criticism, as well as a dominant motif in Dante's *Comedy*.

By the fifth century, the orthodox interpretation of the Scriptures on the one hand, and authoritative church dogma on the other, had reached an accommodation and a fusion of purpose, which presupposed that the Holy Scriptures represented the divinely inspired account of the true and providential course of human history, beginning with man's creation and culminating in the ministry of the Messiah. Such a view was not easily arrived at. It was preceded by interpretive controversies over the method by which the unity of the Scriptures could be established. Clearly the most difficult problem requiring solution was the relationship between the Old and New Testaments. What were the specific features, other than the Truth of their Divine origin, which could cement a vast array of heterogeneous poetic styles and genres into a single whole? Such questions were bound to produce a continual interplay between religious, literary and rhetorical points of view. Self-contained books of the Bible like *Job* and *Ecclesiastes*, the stories of Cain and Abel, Noah and his Ark, Joseph and his brothers, as well as the dramatic episodes which highlight phases in the life of Jesus — all these have the earmarks of story-telling, a concern with beginnings, middles and endings. But was there a larger and more essential story running through the two Testaments? Indeed, was there a story greater than each of the two Testaments taken by itself? Was there an unbroken thread stretching from *Genesis* to *Revelation*? The strenuous efforts exerted toward providing an affirmative answer to this question can be readily observed in medieval interpretations of the Scriptures.

The "Figura" article by Erich Auerbach[1] was a watershed in Dante criticism, indispensible to all those interested in the historical connections between an ingenious interpretive method applied to the Scriptures since the earliest days of the Christian era, and Dante's great epic poem. We will touch on the highlights of Auerbach's essay and then explore the relationship between the "figural" style and the nature of time in the *Comedy*.

The word *figura* (from the same stem as *fingere* and *effigies*), which earlier had meant "plastic form," occasionally attached itself to new meanings during the first century before Christ. Most notably, the theologian Tertullian (c.160-210 A.D.) made use of a by then long-standing semantic opportunity thus becoming the first important Christian thinker to employ the word in an unequivocally new sense, which proved to be of great value to the developing doctrinal norms as applied to Holy Writ. In the context of the polemic tract *Adversus Marcionem*, directed against a fellow-Christian adversary, Tertullian made reference

---

[1] Erich Auerbach, "Figura," in *Scenes from the Drama of European Literature*, trans. Ralph Manheim (New York, 1959), pp. 28-34.

to the biblical personage of Oshea, the son of Nun, and observed that Moses gave him the name of "Iehoshua," or "Joshua" (Num. 13:17). From this he concluded that "For the first time Joshua is called Jesus. . . . This then, we observe, was a 'figure' of things to come (*Hanc primus dicimus figuram futurorum esse*)."[2]

The equation Joshua-Jesus amounts to a prophecy, because the true meaning of the name Joshua can be seen by the believer to lie in its phonetic foreshadowing of Jesus. By the fourth century the old sense of *figura* had almost entirely disappeared from Christian texts. Most influentially, St. Augustine urged its use — in its new meaning of pre-figuration — for sermons and missionary activities. Thus Adam and Moses became "figures" of Christ, and Noah's Ark a figure of the Church. Gradually, and ingeniously, all the important personages in the Old Testament came to be interpreted in this manner, and when the Church Fathers were in need of justification for such departures from literalness, they found it readily in the Pauline Epistles in which the Apostle advocated an interpretation of the Old Testament which differed greatly from that given it by the Jews. According to Paul, an impenetrable veil would cover the Bible whenever the children of Israel read it. They could therefore not hope to understand its true meaning. To a Christian, on the other hand, it would be apparent that Adam was the figure and promise of the Christ to come:

> But their minds were blinded: for until this day remaineth the same vail untaken away in the reading of the old testament; which vail is done away in Christ.
> But even unto this day, when Moses is read, the vail is upon their heart. (II Cor. 3:14-15.)

The sacrificial slaughter of animals found its fulfillment in the sacrifice of Christ's blood (Heb. 9:12), and that which befell the Jews in the Old Testament happened to them as "figures of themselves" (I Cor. 10:11).[3]

By virtue of their concreteness and by the authority of their attested Truth, historical accounts in the Bible have retained the authenticity of sensuous experience. But an earth-bound realism, after all, supports only one aspect — probably no more than a necessary minimum — of these accounts when they are considered as the literally recorded, or

---

[2] Auerbach, "Figura," p. 28.

[3] Where Paul used the Greek work *typos*, St. Augustine and theologians after him invariably rendered it as *figura* in their Latin translations. The word "example" in the King James translation, and the word "warning" in the Revised Standard edition, lack the accuracy and historical resonance of *figura*. The German *Vorbild*, of Lutheran vintage, has the advantage of being both the most literal and the most amenable to the sense which the Church Fathers had come to give to *figura*.

symbolically rendered, Word of God. Even non-biblical historical events must transcend themselves in order to fit into the medieval conception of providential history, and they can best do so when they are understood in their figural relationship to each other, thereby suggesting a pattern of eternal perfection which leaves its imprint throughout the success of historical events. In this perspective, an event which is perceived in relationship to itself alone is incomplete and defective in meaning.

Even the New Testament is a "figure" and therefore short of perfection because it does not reflect or represent; rather, it points to the Kingdom of God; it leads to, but does not inhabit, the end of time. The gulf between the enactment of history and the timeless perfection of eternity can be bridged only by mystical transport, or else by the mediatorship of the Universal Church. The City of God, prophesied and prefigured, is the goal of history to be attained at the end of time; yet even though perfection lies forever in the future, it hovers over every one of the "merely" historical moments. In Auerbach's formulation:

> Figural interpretation establishes a connection between two events or persons, the first of which signifies not only itself but also the second, while the second encompasses and fulfills the first.
> . . . [The figures] are . . . the tentative form of something timeless; they point to something that always has been and always will be; they point to something which is in need of interpretation, which will indeed be fulfilled in the concrete furture, but which is at all time present, fulfilled in God's providence which knows no difference in time.[4]

Thus the Roman Empire was the fulfillment of a destiny whose chosen agent was the Trojan hero, Aeneas. His odyssey to glory began with the escape from the ruins of his defeated city and ended with the founding and securing of Rome. And since the composition of the *Aeneid* was itself an historical event comparable in grandeur and significance to the deeds of Aeneas, Virgil had become a kind of prophet-sorcerer for the Middle Ages, endowed with the power to discern the meaning of history, though having been born just before the Christian era, he could not hope to reap salvation from his poetic prescience.[5]

The *Divine Comedy* represents the culmination of the figural tradition in the Middle Ages, and it is as a figural fulfillment of himself that Virgil's role as Dante's guide through the Inferno and up to the pinnacle of Mount Purgatory must be understood. As seer-poet Virgil had been

---

[4] Auerbach, "Figura," pp. 53, 59.
[5] The "Fourth Eclogue" by Virgil was regarded as a prophecy of the coming of the Messiah, similar to Isaiah's prophecy in Is. IX: 6.

Aeneas' guide through Hades and had forged the links of the providential chain by which Romans could think of themselves as anchored in Greek mythology and see their leaders as cast in the mold of Homeric heroes. Rome in turn was, from the medieval perspective, a figure of the Holy Roman Empire. Though Virgil lived irremediably as a pagan, his majestic poetic vision had raised him to the standing of a quasi-Christian. Dante has the Roman poet Statius, who in the first century A.D. had become a Christian, refer admiringly to Virgil as a man "who walks by night and carries the light behind him," and rather than giving aid to himself, "made wise those who followed him."

> Facesti come quei che va di notte,
> che porta il lume dietro e se non giova,
> ma dopo se fa le persone dotte.[6]

In the context of the metaphysical certainties articulated and embodied by the medieval Church, the access to a transcendent realm was not yet barred by an impassable Pascalian void, nor was human knowledge restricted to the limited range of impressions conveyed by the senses. In the Middle Ages, to speak with T.S. Eliot, "men still had visions,"[7] and hence the circles of the Inferno, the terraces of Purgatory, and the spheres of the Paradiso could be evoked by the mind's eye both as stages of an inward journey and as a projection of objective Truth. The narrator's pilgrimage proceeds not only through the envisioned geography of the three other-worldly realms, but also through a network of structural correspondences. Each major occurrence can be singled out in terms of its immediate poetic function and also for the manner in which it functions as a figuration of the overall design. When as readers or critics we arrest the action and dwell on an image as on a single frame of a motion picture, we are able to discern those features which necessarily give it its particular place with respect to the Primal Light, and to perceive how it "means" by virtue of its demonstrable rapport with The Ultimate.

Just as human history in its Christian interpretation was seen as moving through divinely ordained stages to its end in the Apocalypse, so too the progressive levels of the *Comedy* were seen as leading up toward an absolute religious and poetic fulfillment. Most personages in the *Comedy* are endowed with figural significance even outside the poem, and their role in its "plot" allows them to unfold their mediating role. Thus Virgil acts out the emblematic pattern imposed on him by medieval Christianity; and the pagan Cato, the stern guardian at the foot of

---

6 *Purg.*, XXII, 67-69.
7 *Selected Essays* (New York, 1950), p. 204.

Mount Purgatory, is the figural and Christian fulfillment of the pre-Christian political freedom for which he stood.[8] Near the end of the *Comedy*, as Dante ascends from the Primum Mobile to the Empyrean and beholds the River of Light, Beatrice, in words reminiscent of the passage we cited from the Second Epistle to the Corinthians,[9] explains to her charge how figural interpretation is natural to the purified and exalted Christian vision:

> . . . Il fiume e li topazii
> ch'entrano ed escono e 'l rider dell' erbe
> son di lor vero umbriferi prefazii.
>
> Non che da sè sian queste cose acerbe;
> ma è difetto della parte tua,
> che non hai viste tanto superbe.
>
> . . . The river and the topaz-gems
> That enter and leave it, and the smiling grasses
> Are but a shadowy preface of their truth.
>
> Not that those things are themselves imperfect,
> But the defect is in yourself
> Because your vision has not yet been thus exalted.

> (*PURG.* XXX, 76-81)[10]

The upward direction of successive figural realizations presupposes the existence, above and beyond time, of a pattern of ultimate reality. This is true of biblical and sacred history and applicable with equal force to the *Divine Comedy*. It means that the successive moments of its fable, meticulously plotted by means of astronomical markers (and all history which passes through the pilgrim's poetic consciousness) exist simultaneously and eternally in the highest regions. It is a voyage through time into timelessness, and through time-bound language to the divine Logos. Signs and allusions to the timeless moment and to the dimension-less point abound in Dante's poem. Most notably it appears as the center of a circle, the versatile emblem of Christian geometry.

The opening lines, "Nel mezzo del cammin di nostra vita," are at once very general and very specific. They refer to a time of being lost somewhere near the middle years; and understood in this way they are not far removed from the relaxed imprecision of everyday parlance. But the words gain power and compel close attention as the reader makes

---

[8] For a discussion of Cato's role in the *Divine Comedy*, see Auerbach, pp.65-67, and Robert Hollander, *Allegory in Dante's 'Commedia'* (Princeton, 1969), pp. 123-129.

[9] See p. 57 above.

[10] This and the following translations from the *Divine Comedy* are mine.

the discovery that the "mezzo del cammin" is indeed the precise mid-point in the life of Dante, the pilgrim-narrator of the poem, as well as of Dante, the historical personage. For in the year 1300, the year of the visionary journey, the biographical person of Dante was thirty-five, which is half the biblically allotted life-span of "three score years and ten" (Psalms 90:10). The season is Spring; the sun is at the equinox, the mid-point of its vernal orbit, and all aspects of the spiritual universe are prepared for the poet's descent and subsequent upward pilgrimage on the anniversary of the Resurrection.

The words "mezzo del cammin," moreover, can be seen as an antici-pation of the universal negative center, the place of the utmost gravity at the bottom of the infernal pit. And for those inclined to analogical thinking, they will in good time evoke the ultimate center as well —the node of light in the region above and beyond the celestial spheres.

In the second canto, just before guiding Dante down the "deep and savage road," the shade of Virgil explains the reason for his emergence from Limbo:

> e donna mi chiamo beata e bella
> tal che di comandar io la richiesi.
>
> (*INF*. II, 53-54.)
>
> a lady called on me, so blessed
> and so fair
> that I begged her to command me.

He refers to the soul of Beatrice residing in the highest reaches of the Ptolemeic heavens and tells how, in response to Dante's great love, she was moved to intercede on his behalf. She willed that the beloved should undertake the journey through the three realms even while still among the living. Virgil tells Dante how, in his confinement in Limbo, together with other great pagan souls, he was spellbound by the approaching light of Beatrice's eyes whose radiance preceded the sound of her angelic voice: "Lucevan li occhi piu che la stella" ("Her eyes shone brighter than the stars") (*Inf*. II, 55).

The comparison of the beloved lady's eyes to stars might have been borrowed from the reservoir of standard poetic diction which was avail-able to the Provençal poets and to the practitioners of the "sweet new style," of whom Dante was one. What is remarkable about this use of the simile is its complicated exactness. It should be recalled that while Dante demurs at the entrance to Hell, Beatrice's abode is among the angelic orders in "The Highest," and beyond the sphere of the fixed stars. Although the entire Paradiso is steeped in light and complete transparency, it is evident that even the divine radiance has gradations. The light grows brighter the higher the planetary or stellar sphere, and is most intense at its source in the Empyrean. As "figures" of divine light, the stars at the end of each of the first two *cantiche* point to the goal of Dante's pilgrimage. They first move into the field of vision as remote points beyond the reach of the intellect. At this level they are not so much phenomena in their own right as markers which direct and comfort Dante and his companion as they emerge from the tenebrous circles of the Inferno: "And then we emerged to see the stars again" ("e quindi uscimmo a riveder le stelle") (*Inf.* XXXIV, 139). Later, at the peak of Mount Purgatory — where Virgil could no longer be Dante's guide — the stars shine upon a more confident pilgrim. After his arduous ascent over the tiers of purgation he becomes worthy of a sojourn in Earthly Paradise where he will be "cleansed and made ready to mount to the stars" ("puro e disposto a salir alle stelle") (*Purg.* XXXIII, 145). And in the last line of the *Comedy*, the experience of ecstasy and astral peace is the fulfillment of the early promise contained in Beatrice's eyes. The ultimate vision of Love is neither *figura* nor prophecy; it is a totally self-contained center where desire is at one with unmediated reality.

As a symbol of divine perfection, the sphere and various lesser modalities of it inform the entire poem, though the Inferno and Purgatorio could hold only imperfect allusions to sphericity. The circular aspects of the funnel of Hell and the cone of Purgatory — the one grooved and the other terraced in reciprocal correspondence — could serve either as reminders of divinely decreed damnation or else as harbingers and figures of spherical bliss. The "heavens" of the planets and fixed stars are the stations whose diminishing materiality toward the outer regions signals the proximate entry into pure spirit.[11]

The twenty-eighth canto shows Dante nearing his destination. Here in the Crystalline, or ninth heaven, he is witness to a symbolic representation of the universe, a spectacle which his mind in transport is able to encompass in an instant. At first he is aware only of its reflection, a single divine spark in the eye of Beatrice which "imparadises" his mind; and when he turns to the fiery source of the image, he finds that the point of overwhelming brightness agrees with its reflection like "music with its measure" (XXVIII, 9). Now the poet stands before the the grandeur of the symbolic world center, of the spiritual pivot about which the heavens revolve:

[11] On sphericity in the *Divine Comedy*, see Romano Guardini, "Die Ordnung des Seins und der Bewegung," in *Dante Alighieri: Aufsätze zur Divina Commedia*, ed. Hugo Friedrich (Darmstadt, 1968), p. 255; Karl Vossler, "Dante als religiöser Dichter," *ibid.*, p. 109; and George Poulet, *The Metamorphoses of the Circle* (Baltimore, 1966), pp. XIII-XVI.

un punto vidi che raggiava lume
acuto si, che 'l viso ch'elli affoca
chiuder conviensi per lo forte acume;
. . .
Forse cotanto quanto pare appresso
alo cigner la luce che 'l dipigne
quando 'l vapor che 'l porta più e spesso,
Distante intorno al punto un cerchio d'igne
si girava si ratto, ch'avria vinto
quel moto che più tosto il mondo cigne.

(*PAR.* XXVIII, 16-18; 22-27.)

I saw a point which cast a light so keen
that the eye on which its ray burns
must draw its lid against the piercing power.

Perhaps as closely as a halo appears to gird the light
about that from which it takes its hue,
where the vapor that carries it is most dense,
At such a distance a circle of fire whirled
about the point, it would have outdone the motion
that most swiftly girds the world.

However, despite the brilliance and majesty of the image appearing to Dante in the Crystalline, this model universe is not entirely self-revealing, and the loving intercession of Beatrice is once more required. While the symbolic nature of the whirling concentric spheres is apparent, one aspect of the schema is still beyond the pilgrim's capacity to understand; in fact, it runs counter to all knowledge and faith which he is able to bring to it. In the model before him, the movement of the sphere at the center moves most swiftly, at a speed beyond human conception; the second is proportionately slower, and the outermost sphere — corresponding to the heaven of the fixed stars encircling all the other spheres — revolves most slowly.[12] Yet tradition and the schools had taught him the exact opposite: the lunar sphere, though astronomically at the center, encompasses the imperfect and contingent world of man and is the most sorely affected by the earth's materiality. It must therefore — in moral conformity to its physical situation — revolve at a slow and labored pace. The outermost sphere being on the contrary almost entirely spiritual, would accordingly move most swiftly.

To us, as interpreters of Dante's vision, it becomes clear that the geocentric, Ptolemaic cosmos, and the spiritual and schematic essence of that cosmos, are related to each other by their structural congruence

---

[12] See *Par.* XXVIII, 41-45.

as well as by a kind of compensatory opposition, much like the structural opposition between Inferno and Purgatory. For the poet, the logical tangle is not resolved by Beatrice's response to his inquiry, dealing as it does with ranks of angels and distinctions between the actuality and appearance of virtue. We should note, however, that the design of the world model in the Crystalline is basically in accord with the Plotinian concentric pattern described in the previous chapter, though it is modified and brought into harmony with thirteenth-century doctrine. In the medieval view, on the other hand, the hierarchy of transcendent values was radiantly present in the design of the Ptolemeic universe; the earth was the dominion of the "dark forest," and its center farthest removed from God and the source of all sin. It can readily be seen that this same earth could not also be the world's spiritual center. Such a point must be sought in regions above and beyond the last shadows of materiality.

The poetic use of the non-material sphere, or circle, as a mark of perfection was not new to Dante. It was in just such a sense — though on a far less majestic scale — that he had used it in the earlier *Vita Nuova*, a work in prose with interspersed poems, where in Book XII Love manifests itself in the guise of a white-robed youth. He comes to the poet in a dream, speaking in the Italian tongue, but changes to the solemn tones of Latin when he reveals his divine nature: "Ego tanquam centrum circuli, cui simili modo se habent circumferentiae partes; tu autem non sic" ("I am like the center of a circle to which all points on the circumference have the same relationship; but you are not like that"). However, the disconsolate Dante is not enlightened by this pronouncement. The image is so enigmatic that he asks the youth for an explanation, but receives only the curt reply: "Non domandar più che utile ti sia" ("Do not ask more than is useful to you").[13] Putting aside for the moment its precise meaning within the framework of the *Vita Nuova*, there can be no doubt that this image of the center with its attendant sphere evokes a state of transcendence not accessible to mortals. In the light of its later scope and intensity in the *Comedy*, the use of the image in the *Vita Nuova* appears as a mere youthful experiment.

For the pilgrim of the *Comedy* who has attained to a level beyond the fixed stars, the nest of whirling, "intelligible" spheres brings overwhelming happiness, even though he has not yet reached the source of

---

[13] For varying interpretations of this passage, see Charles Singleton, "Vita Nuova XII: Love's Obscure Words," (*Romantic Review* XXXVI, 1945), pp. 89-102; J.E. Shaw, " 'Ego Tanquam Centrum Circuli Etc.' Vita Nuova, XII" (*Italica* XXIII, 1947), pp. 133-18; Mark Musa, *Dante's Vita Nuova* (Bloomington, 1973), pp. 11, 117; 185.

that bliss which would mark the fulfillment of his quest. On the contrary, the mysterious schema before him fires his high purpose to ascend further. From the Crystalline he moves to the Empyrean, and the radiance of what he is about to behold begins to dominate his mind in transport. The intelligible "model" of the universe recedes, whose center he remembers as "the point which overcame me"; it appears "enclosed by that which it encloses."

> sempre d'intorno al punto che mi vinse
> parendo inchiuso da quel ch'elli 'nchiude,
>
> . . .
> (*PAR.* XXX, 12-13)[14]

Now there is only the River of Light between Dante and the goal of his journey. Its entire length appears to him to join its beginning and end in a perfect circle, the age-old symbol of eternity, and in its midst a point of light without dimension seems to expand into a circle "wider than the sun" (*Par.* xxx, 103-105).

The last canto confirms that the earlier stages of the journey were after all only promises of what lay ahead. Now, in the presence of the Center "the vision is greater than our speech," and "memory fails before so much excess" (*Par.* XXXIII, 56-57). While confessing to his own inadequacy, Dante yet "dared to fix his sight on the eternal light":

> Nel suo profondo vidi che s'interna,
>   legato con amore in un volume,
>   cio che per l'universo si squaderna;
> sustanze e accidenti e lor costume,
>   quasi conflati insieme, per tal modo
>   che cio ch'i' dico è un semplice lume.

> Un punto solo m'è maggior letargo
>   che venticinque secoli alla 'mpresa,
>   che fè Nettuno ammirar l'ombra d'Argo.
> (*PAR.* XXXXIII, 85-90; 94-96)

> In its depth I saw ingathered,
>   bound by love in one volume
>   the scattered leaves of the universe;
> Substance and accidents and their relations,
>   as though fused together in such a manner
>   that whereof I speak is one simple light.

---

[14] The all-encompassing circle is earlier referred to as "non circumscribed" (*non circunscritto*), yet one which circumscribes all (*tutto circunscrive*). *Par.* XIV, 30.

. . .

> One point alone for me makes greater oblivion
> than five and twenty centuries upon the enterprise
> which made Neptune gaze upon the Argo's shadow.

The "punto solo" — here a pinpoint of *time* and not of *space*[15] — is *the source* of the rainbow-like, multiple circles of light, each shining in its own color, each reflecting each, and together forming the single radiance of the Holy Trinity, and with it the effigy of man.

At the beginning of his visionary journey, Dante, the poet and protagonist, found himself "nel mezzo del cammin" — lost at a crude and nebulous midpoint which was neither radiant with hope nor wholly devoid of it. Beneath him, at the nadir of the infernal cone, lay the center of the physical cosmos. Its evil centrality was in polar opposition to, and a travesty of, its divine origin. Later, above the earth's surface, the images of centrality are increasingly transparent and spiritual, and in the Empyrean, *figura* and pure being — or promise and fulfillment — are merged in a single self-sufficient vision. The poetic density in each line of verse, which is less readily available to the consciousness than the dramatic and palpable encounters with the human "shades" in lower places, nevertheless will subliminally affect even those readers who do not engage in detailed textual analysis.

Within the stern constraints of the intertwining *terza rima* and the eleven-syllable line, adhered to throughout the poem, Dante is able to eke out an astonishing poetic latitude. It is as though the poet needed to show that the hard-won freedom gained from service to the self-imposed, exacting Christian discipline, is the only true liberation available to man.

The voyage proceeds through a multiplicity of concretely perceived landscapes and events toward the transcendent simplicity of the divine center. Each event, though dramatically complete in itself, is in a sense prefatory to the whole and holds within it the germ of a higher and more spiritual reality; and the poetry which records the journey's progress correspondingly prefigures its own transcendence. At crucial moments the successiveness of speech is suspended and, as if to signal an irruption of eternity into human discourse, a single expression is repeated in quick succession. The most celebrated example is the inscription over the gate of hell:

---

[15] Dante uses the self-canceling spatial image elsewhere in order to symbolize the abrogation of time, for example: *Par.* XVII, 18 "il punto/a cui tutti li tempi son presenti."

Per me si va nella città dolente,
Per me si va nell'eterno dolore,
Per me si va tra la perduta gente,
Giustizia mosse il mio alto fattore:
Fecemi la divina potestate,
La somma sapienza e'l primo amore.

(*INF*. III, 1-6)

Through me thou goest into the woeful city,
Through me thou goest to eternal pain,
Through me thou goest among the lost people.
Justice moved my Maker on High,
Divine power made me,
Supreme wisdom and primal love.

The lapidary words at the gate of hell announce the lostness of the sinners who must pass under them. The inscription further announces three cardinal attributes of the universal architect: supreme power, ultimate wisdom and primal love. Provided with such a legend, the gateway can be seen not merely as the passageway for those for whom there is no hope, but also as an opening to the entire trans-human vision of the *Commedia*.

In the second circle, the abode of the lustful, where those who sinfully allowed their intellect to be ruled by passion, Paolo and Francesca da Rimini still cling to each other while being tossed about aimlessly by the infernal tempest. When the storm around Francesca is quieted by a higher will, she tells a deeply moved Dante of the event which, while the lovers still possessed their earthly bodies, sealed their damnation. Francesca concludes her story:

Amor, che a nullo amato amar perdona
mi prese del costui piacer sí forte
che, come vedi, ancor non mi abbandona.

(*INF*. V, 103-105)

Love which absolves no one loved from loving
gripped me so strongly with pleasure in him
that, as you see, even now he leaves me not.

Here, even in its illicit and punishable manifestation, love arrests the normal progression of speech. Its threefold sounding in closely linked variations on its semantic root *amor, amato, amar* has such a powerful effect on the poet that he bows his head in grief and falls into a deathlike swoon.

The ascent to the top of Purgatory, the mountain of transition and ever rising hope, proceeds with fewer such repetitions. Except for the fourfold calling out by Dante of the beloved name of Virgil (*Purg.* XXX, 46-51), as the latter ceases to be his guide and returns to his eternal abode in Limbo, there are no examples which are more than incidentally repetitive patterns common to courtly troubador verses and to the *dolce stil nuovo*. Elsewhere reiterations of important words and concepts signal a standing-still, and on occasion serve Dante as semantic allusions to finality; this is precisely what Purgatory does not allow.

From the Earthly Paradise, Dante, now guided by Beatrice, rises into the heavenly spheres. While his mind and senses are still enmeshed in their earthly habits, they cannot yet fully fathom the true nature of the transcendent glow of the images which imprint themselves on his memory. In stark contradiction to the principles of Aristotle's physics concerning the displacement of matter, his bodily self miraculously fuses with the hovering substances about him. In the lowest of the planetary spheres — the sphere of the moon — he encounters the first souls in bliss and, smitten by their diaphanous luminosity, fails to recognize their real existence, He falls into an error opposite to the one which "ignited" Narcissus. Never having seen his own image, the youth of Greek mythology had become enamored with his own insubstantial reflection facing him from the pool by which he was sitting and paid with his life, while passionately embracing his spectral self. Dante records:

> . . .
> per ch'io dentro all'error contrario corsi
> a quel ch'accese amor tra l'omo e 'l fonte.
>
> (*PAR.* III, 17-18)

> . . .
> at which I ran into the opposite error
> to that which ignited love between the
> youth and the spring.

In earthly life it is indeed common to confuse mere reflections with reality. Here in the heavens the opposite is true. What appear as reflections to the still uncomprehending Dante, turn out to be an aspect of a new kind of radiant reality, for they are the souls themselves enshrined in the glow of their own beatitude. Their existence is of a higher order o. reality than that of the living Dante. Narcissus, who had lived as a pagan in pagan times, could not hope to see that Christian reality. This boon could only be granted to the poetic vision of a medieval Christian like Dante.

This reference to a mistaken interpretation of the mirrored self constitutes a turning point with regard to an important aspect of the *Commedia*'s poetic diction. Whereas before, the repetition of key words was isolated and almost incidental to the mainstream of the action, it now becomes more frequent and ever more important as the journey proceeds upward. Having risen to Venus, the fourth and last of the spheres affected by traces of the earth's shadow, Dante encounters those souls which, though cleansed of their human passions and granted heavenly bliss, still fall short of the perfections associated with the spheres which revolve above: the Sun, Mars, Jupiter, Saturn, and the Heaven of the Fixed Stars. Here, in the sphere of Venus, Dante sees Folco, a famous troubador and lover, who in contrition over his past life of dissipation had become a penitent. He had joined a monastic order and embraced its discipline with such ascetic ardor that he soon received the call to be a bishop. Overcome by the radiance surrounding Folco's soul in heaven, Dante addresses him thus:

> "Dio vede tutto, e tuo veder s'inluia,"
> diss'io, "beato spirto, si che nulla
> voglia di sè a te puot'esser fuia."
>
> (*PAR.* IX, 73-75)
>
> "God sees all, and thy seeing in-Hims itself,
> blessed spirit," I said, "so that no desire
> can hide itself from thee."

and then he concludes:

> "Già non attendere' io tua dimanda,
> s'io m'intuassi, come tu t'inmii."
>
> (*PAR.* IX, 80-81)
>
> "I would not await thy question [regarding
> what I just said]
> If I in-theed myself as thou in-meest thyself.

Thus, by means of a violent and almost reckless breeching of the frontiers of accepted diction, the discrete presence of Folco's soul is made to fuse with the divine essence of which it is an aspect. While coinages like "in-me-ing," "in-thee-ing" and "in-him-ing" effectively reflect such a fusion, they are also part and parcel of a linguistic transcendence, a doubling back of words upon themselves, alluding, as it were, to the goal of a single and ultimate *logos*.

In a still higher sphere, Dante creates a pattern of multiplicity by means of a familiar experiment in optics. He reminds the reader that mirrors which are arranged to face one another at such angles that the "primal light," reflected in the first and then re-reflected in the next, will produce an unending series of images, all of them dependent upon their primal, unreflected source.

> Vedi l'eccelso omai e la larghezza
> dell' eterno valor, poscia che tanti
> speculi fatti s'ha in che si spezza,
> uno manendo in sè come davanti.
>
> (*PAR.* XXIX, 142-145)

> See now the height and the breadth
> of the eternal worth, since it has made for itself
> so many mirrors in which it is broken,
> yet remaining one within itself, as before.

Here the phenomenon of replication signals the proximity of the outer limits of human comprehension. Characteristically, the approach to the highest boon is made the more striking since it is accompanied by a reference to an appurtenance which was as common to domestic life as the use of the Tuscan vernacular.

But when Dante enters the Empyrean and begins to behold the glow of the universal center, which in his words "seems enclosed by that which it encloses" (*Par.* xxx, 12), the poet avidly reaches for words that might, without the mediation of metaphor, direct the intellect to the goal of the journey. The lines cited below give evidence of the most arduous poetic labor, but at the same time they convey a sense of the freedom that accrues to one who has emerged from the impediments and frailties of his human condition.[16] Three centrally important words — Light, Love and Joy — occur twice in only five lines:

> . . . 'Noi siamo usciti fore
> [. . .] al ciel ch'è pura luce:
> luce intellettüal, piena d'amore;
>   amor di vero ben, pien di letizia;
>   letizia che trascende ogni dolzore.'
>
> (*PAR.* XXX, 38-42)

> . . . We have come forth
> [. . .] to the heaven that is pure light:
> intellectual light, full of love;
>   love of true good, full of joy;
>   joy that surpasses all sweetness.

The three closely linked abstractions — luce, amore, letizia — serve as a distillate of transcendency. If the "intellectual light" in its purity is

---

[16] For the most illuminating comment on the complex and sometimes harsh coherences in certain passages of the *Commedia*, see Erich Auerbach, *Dante, Poet of the Secular World* (Chicago, 1961), pp. 167-169.

indeed a metaphor, then it is a metaphor for the impossibility of metaphor. The verses in the last canto move along a frontier where poetry begins to contract into itself and move into a non-temporal, no longer speakable region. Dante marks the moment where human speech begins to fail:

> Da quinci innanzi il mio veder fu maggio
> ch 'l parlar nostro, ch'a tal vista cede,
> e cede la memoria a tanto oltraggio.
>
> <div align="right">(<i>PAR.</i> XXXIII, 55-57)</div>
>
> Thenceforward, what I could see was beyond
> our human speech which fails at such a sight,
> and memory fails at such excess.

Concepts like eternity, on the one hand, and an all-encompassing point of simultaneity, on the other, are aspects of the same mystical transcendency. Yet if the cosmic polarities of hell and heaven are eternal and outside of time, then the halfway point of Dante's journey must mark a transition between the two. In a remarkable essay, Charles Singleton shows the top of Mount Purgatory to be such a point of transition. It is here that in allegorical form the Old and New Testaments appear in a single pageant which holds Beatrice-Christ triumphantly in its midst. Singleton writes: ". . . if we will but consider the whole of the *Comedy* as an action, we shall see that at either end of that action, we are outside of time. . . . And now we see that when Beatrice comes, she comes at the center of the stretch in time. It is as if the procession at the center, in so far as that could suggest in its unfolding the whole extent of time, had also held out the symbol of this."[17]

At the goal of the journey which carried Dante from the confinement of the human condition through ever higher stations of purgation and rarefaction lies absolute freedom in absolute obedience to God.

In the Plotinian and early Christian sphere, the regions of transient, earthly phenomena were relegated to the periphery. The infinitely small yet all-encompassing center sent its radiance to the discrete segments of materiality which make up the distant circumference. Such a design was clearly not a replica of the physical universe. Neither for Plotinus nor for St. Augustine nor for St. Thomas Aquinas could the spiritual center reside in the dark mass of the earth. That center had to be luminous, ideal and eternal. However, the imperfect world of mass and of contingencies — including that of the poet's own physical person — also existed and indefeasibly had to serve as the tangible ground through

---

[17] "Pattern at the Center," *Commedia* (Cambridge, Mass., 1954), pp. 57-58.

which, and beyond which, the visionary voyage had to lead into the realm of pure intelligibility. The center of the earth and the center of the universe are thus related not by any similarity, but rather by the geometric exactitude of their opposition. It is an archetypal polarity which generates other contrasting pairs, such as darkness and luminosity, opacity and transparency, paralysis and absolute agility, a list which could be extended almost at will.

The distinction between body and spirit is consistently upheld in the *Comedy*, and the dramatic potential inherent in a scenario where the hero-narrator is the only flesh-and-blood personage among the multitudes of insubstantial souls or "shades," gives rise to poetic wonderment, and occasionally approaches the limits of assent on the part of modern readers. Sometimes Dante is immediately recognized for the spatial and temporal being that he is, or else a damned soul will learn the truth indirectly — and the reader coincidentally will be reminded of that truth — by means of certain tell-tale signs of a bodily presence: for example, the emblematic boat, on which the ill-tempered Phlegyas swiftly conveys the weightless souls across the river Styx to the lower circles of Hell, sinks deeply into the foul waters when Dante steps into it from the safety of the upper bank; or the scene on Mount Purgatory where, unlike all the non-material presences engaged in their upward progression, the poet's body blocks the sun's rays and casts a sharply defined shadow across the pathway before him.

The goal of the pilgrim's ascent through the planetary spheres is the non-dimensional point of pure spirituality, the "center" which was "figured" in Beatrice's eyes. The quality of "infinity" was not yet functional in the circular image of God in its Augustinian and Thomistic versions; the neo-Platonic "intellectual" sphere was still part of the medieval Christian repertoire, and for Dante as well, the periphery was a lesser version of the center. But with the advent of the word "infinity" in *The Book of Twenty-Four Philosophers*, it became possible to construct a cosmology in which physical and spiritual qualities were no longer at war with one another — or at least could enjoy a prolonged armistice. As the circular image was channeled through the mysticism of Eckhart and through the geometric symbolism of de Cusa, the ideal form of the Universe, and its imperfect manifestations on earth and in the skies, became merely different aspects of a single divine vestment. Using Eckhart's new formulation — in turn based on *The Book of Twenty-Four Philosophers* — de Cusa later saw the center in the divinely inspired soul of man, thus creating a lasting paradigm for Renaissance creativity. The Copernican heliocentric solution to the increasingly intractable problems of planetary motions, the polycentric worlds of Giordano Bruno — these would later be seen as structural aspects of an infinite universe, because "infinity" could comprise concrete phenomena in a way that the older Plotinian "intelligibility" could not. After Dante, the association between matter and evil began to weaken.

Beginning with the first line of Dante's epic, a vision of centrality becomes a thematic as well as a structural part of the *Comedy*. It subsequently appears in many guises, and its moral attributes range from total evil to total good. In all three *cantiche*, the "middle" is ever present, precisely in the manner of the Scriptures, where a divine will is non-temporally active at each historical juncture of its providential progression. It is not merely a matter of an image central to the *Commedia*, but of an image which, in its own right and outside the poem, is a remarkable correlative of an all-encompassing centrality. In the Bible, an over-arching present tense hovers over a long chain of successive historical events. But events and personages in themselves — for example, the building of Noah's Ark, the story of Jacob and Isaac, the Exodus from Egypt — these are all rungs on a ladder which lead toward fulfillment in a non-historical, eternal present. While the personages act out their lives, and the events "take place" (and take time) in biblical history, neither are so constituted as to be in and of themselves aspects of an eternal present. In order to allocate to them a place in the scheme of eternity, it is necessary that we interpret them as *figurae*; for when the power of Erich Auerbach's special optic is brought to bear upon our reading of the *Comedy*, we can see — and even feel — how the seven days of Dante's visionary voyage and how the successive encounters with the shades of the departed, proceed under the dominance of an eternal simultaneity (see pp. 55-58).

In the *Comedy* the geometric images of centrality are capable of immediately yielding the meaning of their intrinsic symbolic structure, though, to be sure, the variant versions of the circle-and-center appear to be arrayed in keeping with the traditional figural progression. As well as pointing to or prefiguring higher realizations of themselves, the circle-center images, unlike *figurae*, can reveal — without the mediation of history — the essence of that to which they point. They are symbols of a timeless presentness transcending history and also transcending the temporal aspect of human language. With the dimensionless "node of light" in the Empyrean, the image has reached its perfection. Here structure and meaning are one. For those able to behold it, the center holds within itself a self-revealing world in all its historical particularity. It is the ultimate Concrete Universal.

Chapter Four

GOETHE'S *FAUST*: AN ALCHEMIST'S WAGER

If ever I should tell the moment
Oh stay! You are so fair!
Then you may cast me into chains,
Then I will smile upon perdition.

GOETHE, *FAUST I*

During the great intellectual wave of the Enlightenment, a new confidence in the sovereign power of human reason swept through the intellectual centers of Europe. Reason and common sense became the sole legitimate interpreters of the physical universe. Thinkers in the early eighteenth century, buoyed by a boundless optimism regarding the analytic powers of enlightened minds, were putting some distance between their philosophy and the once binding tenets of religious dogma. On similar grounds, mystical insights into the nature of time and eternity had lost their relevance, and since "eternal moments" were not intellectually accessible, they became pseudo-problems or insubstantial fantasies. Thus poetry became a likely ambience for dealing with transcendent matters imaginatively and harmlessly, and it could do so without detriment to itself, whether it dealt in religious terms, or in the more worldly currencies of poetic diction.

As a child in Frankfurt and as a university student in Leipzig, Goethe duly respected and adopted the outlook of his learned elders and role models. He admired Voltaire and Diderot and felt indebted to Lessing who was born only twenty years before him. But as a twenty-four-year-old law student who enjoyed writing poems and plays and who was not very interested in jurisprudence, he became impatient with the neo-classical rules of literary decorum, which to him seemed like superannuated impositions on free spirits like his fellow students, and above all on a person like himself. With a growing awareness of his own poetic powers and under the tutelage of the older Herder, he eagerly shed, along with the other Stormers and Stressers, the ballast of the old poetics, so that the first major dramatic product of this period, the historical drama *Götz von Berlichingen* (1773) — much beholden to Shakespearean tragedy — was so out of keeping with prevailing dramatic practice that the young poet, fresh out of the Strasbourg law school, took care not to have his name appear on the title page of the first, privately printed edition. And certainly among the most important themes of *The Sorrows of Young Werther* (1774), Goethe's first novel, was the conflict between reason — or rather reasonable behavior — and the all-or-nothing demands of the heart. The hero's values — and Werther himself — could not survive in a society organized along rationalistic principles. Yet while feeling was beginning to take precedence over ratiocination among influential literary groups and movements, not all traditional norms were thereby abandoned. While, for example, the now discredited convention had dictated that the coherence and verisimilitude of a dramatic work had to be sustained and ratified by the unities of time, place and action, the necessity for unity as such was not doubted by the new generation, but it was seen in quite a new light. And it therefore became less and less acceptable to invoke — on behalf of an abstract principle of unity — the authority of a poetics whose prescriptive norms had been irreparably undermined by the new vehement reliance on unclassifiable, quasi-oracular promptings.

Yet unity, however constituted, was still a condition of a work's existence as a meaningful verbal structure, though it became apparent during the latter part of the eighteenth century that the demand for it could no longer be satisfied by an observance of the old "unities." The time was ripe for the emergence of new principles which would inform and unify a work from within, and perhaps the most important single source for the emergence of such new principles was Edward Young's *Conjectures on Original Composition* (1759). While it found only a modest response in England, in Germany it quickly received a warm welcome. There the essay was translated twice within two years of its publication and did not fail to influence the Stormers and Stressers in the 1770's.[1] While it does not specifically address the problems of unity and coherence in literature, its most famous passage served to place the issue into an entirely new context:

---

[1] Cf. M.H. Abrams, *The Mirror and the Lamp* (New York, 1953), pp. 201-202; also Lilian R. Furst, *Romanticism in Perspective* (New York, 1969), pp. 30-31.

An original may be said to be of a vegetable nature; it rises spontaneously from the vital root of genius, it is not made.[2]

Goethe went far beyond his contemporaries in embracing the new organicism. While others borrowed from living nature such general concepts and expressions as growth, bloom, or fruition, and while they preferred metaphors like these to the mechanistic and architectonic ones used by their elders, Goethe expended enormous energy on studies and observations in biology and several other fields of natural science. The principles which he developed as an enthralled observer of biological nature could at times become informing principles of his poetry. Similarly, some of his concepts of color theory and geology found their way into his poetry either topically or as structural elements.[3]

Goethe was a voracious reader. His intellect ranged over many fields of knowledge; his sensibility was militantly undivided and responded to the arts and to natural science with equal fervor, so that in the eyes of his admirers he became a "Renaissance man" of the eighteenth century. Nothing much eluded him except mathematics, which he regarded with distaste; he steadfastly held to his belief that there was a lack of compatibility between living nature and mathematical modes of thought. "What is exact about mathematics, except its own exactitude?" stands as a rhetorical question among other entries in his notebooks dealing with natural philosophy. Mathematical theories and hypotheses seemed to Goethe "cradle songs with which teachers lull their students to sleep."[4] In the course of his futile struggle against the "unnatural" Newtonian edifice of a mathematically explicable and coherent universe, he attempted to lay the groundwork for a non-mathematical and reverential approach to its secrets. For him, the intuitions of the poet and the insights of the natural scientist were closely related and should be regarded as facets of the same creative imagination. The poetic vision implicit in Goethe's treatises on plant morphology and color theory were never at odds with what was meant to be its scientific truth. His natural science gave body and strength to his poetry, and his poetic faculty gave to his scientific writings a quality of controlled sensuous involvement. Knowledge for Goethe was not to be gained by standing aloof from the observed phenomenon, but by developing a sympathetic and imaginative rapport with it. Moreover he practiced, described, and continuously

---

[2] E. Young, *Conjectures on Original Composition*, ed. E.K. Morley (Manchester, 1918), p. 8.

[3] Several such concepts, though not based on vegetable life, can yet be shown to be "biologically" oriented. Cf. my *The Poem as Plant: A Biological View of Goethe's Faust* (Cleveland, 1971).

[4] This and the preceding quotation are translated by me from *Jubiläumsausgabe* XXXIX, pp. 73, 76. All following translations in this chapter are mine.

urged an approach to nature that would maintain the integrity of each of its manifestations. Factuality would thus somehow yield its own "theory" and would not be blurred or falsified by intervening filters of abstraction:

> The highest boon would be to understand that all facts are already theory. The blue of the sky reveals to us the basic chromatic laws. If we could only stop looking for things behind the phenomena: they themselves are the theory.[5]

Under favorable circumstances, it might be possible for a highly advanced sensibility to come upon the workings of nature with such imaginative participation as to be face to face with a basic pattern underlying and informing a multitude of particular manifestations. The most celebrated example of such an archetypal form is Goethe's *Urpflanze*, the prototypal plant which he had envisioned while observing certain luxuriant specimens in the botanical gardens of Palermo in Sicily. The excitement elicited in him by such a discovery can be felt in this segment of his letter to a beloved friend, Frau von Stein:

> The archetypal plant will be the strangest creature in the world; nature herself should be envious of it. With this model and the key to it one is in a position to invent an infinity of plants which will have to be consistent with one another, that is to say, even if they do not exist, they yet could exist, not at all as picturesque or poetic shadows but containing an inner truth and necessity.   (June 9, 1787)

Such a leaf-like configuration should not be thought of as existing in any material sense. It is a schema from which concretely existing forms can be derived. The pattern is instantly present to the mind and contains "actually and potentially," in Goethe's words, all possible variants of dicotyledonous plants.

The archetypal plant is both poetic science and scientific poetry. Its "idea" on the one hand, and its tangible existence on the other, are irreversibly fused by "action" (*handeln*), a creative dynamism which for Goethe was above all the making of poetry:

> Theory and practice are in steady conflict with one another — whatever union between them can be effected by reflection is illusory; only action can unite them.[6]

In other words, it is not the function of the poet to exemplify general ideas by means of appropriate facts, nor does he engage in a process of

---

[5] *Jub.* XXXIX, p. 72.
[6] *Jub.* XXX, 391.

arranging facts in order to support some pre-existing idea. Rather he is bent on achieving what is rationally impossible: the complete fusion of opposite poles of human experience. Since facts exist in time, and ideas exist above and beyond time, poetry resides on a level of imaginative reality where successiveness and simultaneity are held together in a momentary and fragile union. This is one sense in which the making of a unified poetic work must always involve a struggle with temporality. In the meditative essay "Misgivings and Acceptance" (*Bedenken und Ergebung*), included in a work on plant and animal morphology, Goethe wrote:

> The difficulty of combining idea and experience is an obstacle in all of natural science: the idea is independent of space and time; for this reason, simultaneity and successiveness are intimately conjoined in the idea, but from the point of view of experience, forever separate; and a set of occurrences in nature, which in accordance with the idea we should think of as being at once simultaneous and successive, seems to produce in us a kind of derangement. Reason cannot unite that which the senses have delivered to it separately, and thus the quarrel between sense perception and abstration remains forever unresolved.
>
> Hence we take some pleasure in making good our escape into poetry . . .[7]

Indeed the heart of the *Faust* poem can be seen as a symbol of this struggle. The wager between Faust and Mephistopheles is for the highest possible stake: an all-encompassing moment of existence, the most absolute imaginable unity of all experience:

> Werd' ich zum Augenblicke sagen:
> Verweile doch! du bist so schön!
> Dann magst du mich in Fesseln schlagen,
> Dann will ich gern zugrunde gehn! (1699-1702)

> If ever I should tell the moment:
> Oh stay! You are so fair!
> Then you may cast me into chains,
> Then I will smile upon perdition!

Perhaps Faust, who is also a translator of the Bible, remembers that in the fourth chapter of the Gospel of Luke it was Satan who had tempted Jesus with a similar offer:

---

[7] *Ibid.*

And the devil, taking him up into an high mountain, showed unto him all the kingdoms of the world in a moment of time. And the devil said unto him, All this power will I give thee, and the glory of them: for that is delivered unto me: and to whomever I will give it.
If thou therefore will worship me, all this shall be thine.[8]

"All the kingdoms of the world in a moment of time" — this moment, a mere pinprick, translated from the Greek *stigme chronou*, is the most irresistible gift offered to man. In both Luke and Goethe's *Faust*, it is offered by the devil and is illicit because it usurps the prerogative of divinity. Unlike Jesus, Faust accepts the temptation in a desperate thrust toward the absolute. His ambition is both sinful and sacred: sinful, because in following it he allies himself with Evil; and sacred, because it gives testimony to his thirst for a share of divinity. In the end, Goethe allows his hero to be saved despite his guilt, or rather because of it.

The "moment", or "Augenblick", is not only the fulcrum of the dramatic action in *Faust*; it is also a vehicle for Goethe to probe the limits of poetry. It is precisely in the dimensionless point — and only there — that experience and idea, practice and theory, concreteness and abstraction are fused into a seamless unity. It is the center of the infinite sphere, although sphericity in Goethe does not appear in concentric bundles or in radial rapport with the center. Instead circles and pinpoints appear separately and successively in such a way that their completion occurs retroactively in the reader's mind.

Neither circularity nor centrality are symbolic of the Lord alone. They appear typically at both poles of the Judeo-Christian transcendency, and when Mephistopheles makes his first appearance as a poodle, Faust says to his factotum Wagner:

Bemerkst du, wie in weitem Schneckenkreise
Er um uns her und immer näher jagt? (1152-53)
. . .
Der Kreis wird eng, schon ist er nah! (1162)

See how in ample spiral turns
It streaks about us, drawing ever closer?
. . .
The circle tightens; the creature is close by!

Finally the poodle reveals itself as an emissary from Hell, while Faust in his study pores over a German translation of the Gospel of John. Looking up from his labors he mockingly addresses his new companion:

---

[8] This passage was pointed out to me by Herbert S. Long, Professor of Classics at Case Western Reserve University, and I gratefully acknowledge my debt to him.

Das also war des Pudels Kern! (1323)
So this was the poodle's core!

Here Goethe makes clever use of a well-worn German phrase conveying
the pleasurable sensation that accompanies a sudden unexpected insight
into the nature of a thing — a meaning that might be approximated in
English by: "so that's what it boils down to!" But readers and spectators
who have been alerted by the poodle's fire-trailing, spiraling approach
to his prey, will see that "the poodle's core" is also the center of an
infernal circle.

Such an interpretation is retroactively reinforced by later circular
images in the context of infernal goings-on. For example, in the Witch's
Kitchen, where Faust is to drink the potion that will give him youthful
good looks, we hear Mephisto tell the presiding witch:

Zieh deinen Kreis, sprich deine Sprüche,
Und gib ihm eine Tasse voll! (2530-2531)
Draw your circle, speak your spells,
Give him a gobletful of brew!

a command with which, according to the ensuing stage direction, the
hag eagerly complies.

Circularity appears with greater amplitude and luminosity outside the
earthly limits which surround the first part of the drama. In the "Prel-
ude in Heaven," which precedes the human course of events, the archetypal antagonists reach agreement regarding the action yet to be played
out on earth. The archangel Raphael opens the celestial assembly by
chanting words in praise of the glories of the universe:

Die Sonne tönt nach alter Weise
In Brudersphären Wettgesang,
. . .

The sun intones his ancient song
in contest with fraternal spheres,
. . .

And it is not until the final scene of the Second Part — after Faust's
death — that the action moves again into the heavenly regions where it
all began. As may be expected, this last scene in heaven — a more Cath-
olic abode than the rather unitarian ambiance of the Prologue — again
exhibits circles and spheres — only a few of them — but as indispensable features of the ethereal region: a Pater Seraphicus exhorts a chorus
of Blessed Youths to "rise up to the higher circle" (11918); the Younger

Angels become aware of the Blessed Youths who are "grouped in a circle" (11974); the Mater Gloriosa appears in the midst of a "wreath of stars" (11994) and lovingly beckons to a transfigured Gretchen: "Come! Arise to yet higher spheres!" (12094) — her gesture in turn causing Faust's spirit to be drawn to greater and greater perfection by the power of the Eternal Feminine.

The cosmic wager between the Lord and Satan in the Prologue is the overture to the wager between Faust and Mephisto. In both transactions the stakes go to the heart of the drama's meaning. If Faust, the exemplar of man, can be subverted and seduced into stagnation, he will be given over to Mephisto. Faust enters the wager fully convinced that his life will be to the end a desperate and futile struggle for absolute knowledge, and that the gulf between his grasp and his boundless ambition can never be closed. It is this striving — or *streben* — in the face of hopelessness which in the end moves the heavens to bestow grace on him. Winning the wager would mean a continuous struggle at the edge of despair, the living out of the frustrations of a Faustian life. Losing it, on the other hand, would mean that Mephisto had succeeded in supplying Faust with the ultimate moment, an impermissible situation tantamount to an admission that the arch-antagonist is equal to God as a source of beatitude. Whether in the course of his long life Faust actually attains to the moment, is a matter of continuing critical debate.[9] He certainly comes within sight of it; but whether he possesses it as a living human being is a question clothed by Goethe in cunning subjunctives and rhetorical ambiguities. In any case, the *Augenblick* is the maximum-in-the-minimum, the all-in-one concrete-universal, and has all the paradoxical attributes of the geometric and mystical center-circle imagery which had for so long served as a symbolic representation of eternity and the Christian God's ubiquitous presence.

The wager between Faust and Mephisto spells out, in narrowly legal terms, the relationship between the two, but as the action progresses, the Moment expands its meaning and as it moves closer to Faust's grasp, its nature is refined and its power intensified, in conformity with the expanding quality of Faust's life. The first of Faust's experiences in the company of Mephisto, the easy hoodwinking of the students in Auerbach's Cellar, their vulgar delights and hackneyed posturings, merely bore him. He remains silent — presumably a detached observer — while Mephisto works the untried students' minds into a frenzy of drunken camaraderie; and when they bellow in chorus that they feel "so

9 See for example: Ada Klett, *Der Streit um Faust II seit 1900* (Jena, 1939), pp. 180-200; also Hermann J. Weigand, "Wetten und Pakte in Goethe's *Faust*," *Monatshefte* 53 (December, 1961), 325-337.

good, so cannibalic jolly," Faust curtly dismisses the shallow spectacle as holding no interest for him:

Ich hätte Lust, nun abzufahren. (2296)

I am ready now to leave the scene.

This is a mere preliminary probe of Faust's capacity to evaluate experience in terms of the recently entered wager. Clearly the humid celebrations of good fellowship miss the mark. It is only after a stop in the Witch's Kitchen in order to drink a rejuvenating potion, that Mephisto's offerings take on the aspect of serious temptations. Faust's first encounter with Gretchen, a pretty small-town girl, produces in him an imperious sexual desire. Made irresistible by Mephisto's machinations, Faust's Don Juan-like amorous strategies have their desired effect. Gretchen falls deeply in love, submits to him and becomes pregnant. In the company of Mephisto, Faust ruthlessly and selfishly pursues his goal and in the process becomes implicated in the death of several human beings who stand in his way, and finally in the death of Gretchen as well. Yet the initially purely sensual character of the Moment is gradually heightened and transcended. Its destructive carnality gives way to a more encompassing and generous conception of love.

The first part of *Faust* ends with the tragedy of Gretchen. Faust has ruined an innocent and once self-sufficient life, sacrificed it for the sake of a destiny-fraught, self-centered quest. It is true that in sexual consummation he has touched on the Moment, but it has not brought lasting contentment. The encounter with Gretchen is only one of several possible realizations of a Goethean archetypal pattern. It will generate others, in the same manner that the configuration of a prototypal plant will generate successive metamorphoses of its leaves which become more differentiated and refined from node to higher node, until they attain to their final form as sepals, petals and other parts of the blossom.[10]

Thus Faust "outgrows" the Moment with Gretchen, and in the second part of the drama the action moves into the enormous arena of political life, war and commerce. It is in the third act of *Part II* that a compression of three thousand years into an instant of poetic actuality is attempted. The phantasmagoric encounter between Faust, now the

---

[9] See also for example Heinz Politzer: "Goethe's *Faust* not only grew like a tree during the latter part of his life, but it is also a very symmetrical composition." Quoted from "The Tree of Knowledge and the Sin of Science — Vegetarian Symbols in Goethe's *Faust*," in *Aspects of the Eighteenth Century*, ed. Earl R. Wasserman, (Baltimore, 1965), pp. 281-304. For a more detailed discussion of the relationship between Goethe's biology and poetry, see my *Poem as Plant*.

lord of a medieval castle, and Helen of Troy, conjured up from the Homeric past, is surrounded by a vertiginous "doubling" effect which signals the Moment's immediate proximity.

Much earlier, near the end of the first act of *Part II*, Faust's magic powers had brought forth the phantom of Helena and Paris, and caused the pair to reenact its legendary encounter in silent pantomime before the nobility of the imperial court. In her second appearance, however, Helena is no longer a ghostly and silent apparition, but a concrete dramatic character, aware of her fateful beauty and aware also — through a sort of poetic miracle — of her mythic role in the history of Western man. Before her actual encounter with Faust, she appears in Menelaus' palace. Troy has been sacked; Helen is restored to her husband and to her native land. The nordic Mephisto is uncomfortable and out of place in Greek antiquity, but his presence is felt through the disguise of a lady-in-waiting. He reproaches Helena for her past escapades, including not only those known from Homer and Virgil but from medieval legend as well. Mephisto accuses her of having consorted with Theseus, Patroclus, and Achilles, as well as with Paris. And Helena appears to be aware of her place in human consciousness and of the precarious play of forces upon which her poetic actuality depends. Mephisto exploits the tenuousness of her hold on reality and gains a momentary victory when Helena faints and before our eyes fades into non-being:

> Helena: Verwirre wüsten Sinnes Aberwitz nicht gar.
> Selbst jetzo, welche denn ich sei, ich weiß es nicht.
> (8875-76).
>
> Do not derange completely my distracted wit.
> Even now, whoever I may be, I know it not.

And then as Mephisto presses on, she dissolves into a figment of herself:

> Ich als Idol, ihm dem Idol verband ich mich.
> Es war ein Traum, so sagen ja die Worte selbst.
> Ich schwinde hin und werde selbst mir ein Idol
> (8879-81).
>
> I, as an idol, joined an idol:
> It was a dream, the gods themselves declare it.
> I fade away and now become an idol to myself.

Helena's self-abstraction truly amounts to an identity crisis and reverses the process of poetic integration by exposing, one by one, the layers of a fully realized, dramatic stage presence. The self-conscious distancing from the concrete, temporal self, its excarnation, makes clear the ephemeral quality of this quintessentially poetic moment as a self-revealing mystery.[11] With this, the reader is prepared for the ensuing union between Faust and Helena which brings about the condensation of Western history into an ecstatic present moment:

Helena: Ich fühle mich so fern und doch so nah,
Und sage nur zu gern: Da bin ich! Da!

Faust: Ich atme kaum, mir zittert, stockt das Wort;
Es ist ein Traum, verschwunden Tag und Ort.

Helena: Ich scheine mir verlebt und doch so neu,
In dich verwebt, dem Unbekannten treu.

Faust: Durchgrüble nicht das einzigste Geschick!
Dasein ist Pflicht, und wär's ein Augenblick.
(9411-9418)

Helena: I feel so far away and yet so near,
And all too pleased to say: I'm here! I'm here!

Faust: I scarcely breathe: I tremble, stammer;
It is a dream; gone are place and day.

Helena: I feel myself at once so ancient and so new,
Bound to a stranger, enmeshed in you.

Faust: Brood not upon this rarest of all destinies!
The being-there is duty, if only for an instant.

This union signals a kind of fulfillment which should make it easy for Mephisto to declare himself the winner of the wager. It would be a mistake to conclude, as Wilhelm Emrich does, that the *Augenblick* here is so qualitatively different from the one which was the subject of the wager early in the first part of the drama, that they are in fact not significantly related.[12] The reason for Mephisto's non-intervention must instead be sought in the mythical and explicitly "phantasmagoric" nature of this "Helena act."[13] It does not properly touch the "real" Faust as he is constituted in all other parts of the drama. We know from the Prologue that Mephisto's intended victim must be fully human and confined within established mundane limits.

"Offenbares Geheimnis," an expression used repeatedly by Goethe in reference to both poetry and natural phenomena.

"Nichts aber wäre widergoethescher, als die Feier des Augenblicks mit Faust's Wette in Verbindung bringen zu wollen. . . ." Wilhelm Emrich, *Die Symbolik von Faust II* (Bonn, 1957), p. 343.

In 1827, Goethe published the Helena act separately under the title *Helena. Klassisch-romantische Phantasmagorie. Zwischenspiel zu Faust.*

But fantastic or not, this marriage of nothern man with Greek antiquity conjures up unmistakable signs of the *Augenblick* which owes its special radiance to the conflation of three millennia into the "highest moment." In the same manner that crude sexuality had been raised toward love, that Gretchen's simple prettiness had been transposed into the majestic beauty of Helena, the Moment as well has undergone a process of heightening and intensification.[14]

Now is a good time to take stock of the resemblances between this important aspect of *Faust* and the progressive stages of the pilgrimage through the three realms of Dante's *Commedia*. While the journey downward into the pit took the pilgrim to ever deepening horrors, the subsequent laborious climb along the terraces of Mount Purgatory and the weightless ascent through the heavenly spheres, showed an opposite intensification, a "heightening" transport toward ultimate spiritual fulfillment. The progression in the *Commedia* from foreshadowing to concrete realization, from moments an implicit promise to gloriously overt fulfillment, has been shown by Auerbach to be rooted in biblical exegesis. For Dante, the Christian poet and thinker, history was instilled with Divine providence — and clearly his *sacro poema* is informed by both biblical and worldly history — from Adam to the resurrection of Christ, the new Adam; and from the Trojan roots of Augustan Rome to the Holy Roman Empire of the Middle Ages.

Heightening or *Steigerung* in *Faust* can be related to Goethe's particular understanding of biological processes. Just as his understanding of the growth of individual plants — toward ever greater differentiation culminating in the sepals and petals of the blossom — informed his interpretation of all natural processes, and *Faust* as well, so Dante's Christian epic was illuminated by a mediaeval Thomistic perspective. It should not be surprising therefore that the heightening of the Moment in *Faust* should be structurally comparable to the progressive figural stages leading to the "node of light" in the Empyrean of the *Commedia*. In both works the "center" is a pinpoint of all-encompassing, simultaneous presentness.

The phenomenon of Helena becoming an idol to herself, a ghostly doubling of her presence, has its counterpart in Goethe's scientific observation in the field of optics. He had become interested in "entoptic" images — that is, in certain multiple projections which result when an object is observed through such transparent mineral crystals as mica, selenite and feldspar. The phenomenon clearly fascinated him and, in various guises, entered his poetic productions.

---

[14] The German "Steigerung" denotes both increased intensity and a higher level of perfection.

For example, in the novel with the allusive chemical title *Elective Affinities (Die Wahlverwanschaften)*, published in 1808 when Goethe had nearly completed his monumental tract on the theory of color, there occurs a scene in the course of which an architect had restored a private chapel on a country estate and decorated its ceiling with conventionally painted angels. The architect's efforts took several weeks during which he asked Ottilie, the novel's heroine, not to enter the chapel, so that he might have the pleasure of surprising her with the completed frescoes. He was an unpretentious amateur painter and made no claim for originality. Whether it was that he lacked sufficient skill, or whether he had thus unconsciously expressed his forbidden love for Ottilie, the fact was that each of the assembled angels peering awkwardly from the ceiling, had Ottilie's unmistakable features. When she was finally asked to enter the chapel, her sensation upon seeing her multiplied face crowding in on her from above is rendered in this remarkable passage:

> [Ottilie] stood still, walked back and forth, saw and observed; in the end she sat down on one of the chairs, and it seemed to her, as she looked up and about, as if she did and did not exist, did and did not perceive herself, as if all those things before her should vanish and she vanish to herself; and only when the sun left the window which until then it had brightly illuminated, did Ottilie awaken to her inward self and hurry to the manor. (II, 3)

How important the phenomenon of "entoptic" images was to Goethe can be gathered from a biographical entry written in 1822 and published posthumously. It was inspired by a friend's report of a visit to Sesenheim, an idyllic village near Strasbourg where Goethe, as a young law student, had met and loved Friederike Brion. The concluding paragraph reads:

> If we consider that repeated moral reflections not only keep the past alive, but even intensify it to a higher life, then we will be mindful of the entoptic images which also by no means diminish from mirror to mirror but flash out all the more, then we shall acquire a symbol for events which in the history of the arts and of religion — and probably in the political sphere as well — have occurred repeatedly and are still occurring every day.[15]

Here the multiple images are external objects; for Ottilie and for Helen of Troy they are inwardly experienced reflections; a ghostly simultaneity is suddenly superimposed upon the successive ticking-off of historical events and of the words by which they are articulated.

Remarkably enough, when Dante as the hero and narrator of the *Commedia*, encountered and then crossed over into the poetic and religious regions of unfailing presentness and eternal simultaneity, he too

---

[15] *Jub.* xxv, pp. 222-23.

resorted to repetition and reduplication. There is no evidence whatever, so far as I know, that would suggest any influence of this aspect of Dantean poetic diction on Goethe. Instead, it is likely a case of similarly constituted images which on the instant of their highest intensity, elicited startlingly similar verbal impulses and configurations.[16] Mirror reflections in Dante and the refraction of light in Goethe provide a "down-to-earth" scientific basis — each appropriate to its time — for phenomena which were perceived as mysterious and ghostly in Dante's as much as in Goethe's time. On the other hand, Narcissus' mistaken love for his mirrored self gave a mythological dimension to Dante's inverse experience in the heaven of the moon, while Helen of Troy's inner split between her "real" and mythological selves served Goethe to overcome, phantasmagorically, the linear flow of history.

While Faust searches for ways to break out of the confines of his human nature, and risks all for the sake of the single all-encompassing "pinpoint," the drama itself often dwells lovingly on temporal life as it touches and caresses the senses. There are scenes, such as the "Easter Walk" in *Part I*, and the opening passages of *Part II*, where almost nothing interferes with the sufficiency and contentment derived from the sparkle and plenitude of the immediate surroundings. In *Part II*, in fact, it is as though the poet had given up the notion of a frontal assault. Ruthless aggression — largely sexual in nature — had brought the Faust of *Part I* face to face with his guilt; Gretchen's tragedy was a concomitant of his alliance with Evil.

The more objective mode of *Part II* shows a new trust in the here-and-now. Faust learns that he cannot face the sun directly without being blinded. He must turn away from it and be content to admire the borrowed radiance of the rainbow. It is an indirection — not truth itself — like all symbols; but rather than bringing despair, the shimmering arc in the sky becomes the occasion for a paean on the beauty of the early moments of a new day in Spring. Gone is the old vehemence, and instead of fragmented chunks of raging emotion, one finds marvelously sculptured phrases and a readiness to move along intricate byways of symbolic and allegorical evocation. The advance toward the goal of ultimate experience continues, but it has been transformed from its disastrous, headlong course into a slow, circuitous, and organic progression, remarkably analogous to Goethe's vision of the successive stages in the growth of a plant.

Most significantly, the *Augenblick* itself is recalled during the last hours of Faust's life, and while it resembles the yearned-for moment of the wager of long ago, its structure and meaning have changed. A metaphysical breakthrough into the Absolute is no longer required to achieve

---

[16] See pp. 72-77 above.

it, and it is no longer quite the infinitely small pinpoint carried over from the hermetic and mystical tradition. Instead the *Augenblick* has now become a phase of life, a somewhat expanded moment of personal history. The earlier imperious demand for a share of eternity has faded, and even if the traces of Faust's great works will last for "aeons," as in the lines cited below, they will not last forever. The Moment has become historicized, and Nicolas de Cusa's "maximum in the minimum" has been moderated, as it were, into a "much in little." Faust utters his last words while surveying his vast, newly developed domain:

> Und so verbringt, umrungen von Gefahr,
> Hier Kindheit, Mann und Greis sein tüchtig Jahr.
> Solch ein Gewimmel möcht' ich sehn,
> Auf freiem Grund mit freiem Volke stehn.
> Zum Augenblicke dürft' ich sagen:
> Verweile doch, du bist so schön!
> Es kann die Spur von meinen Erdentagen
> Nicht in Äonen untergehn. —
> Im Vorgefühl von solchem hohen Glück
> Genieß' ich jetzt den höchsten Augenblick.
> (11577-11586)

> And thus the child, the man, and then the patriarch,
> They all traverse the dangerous corridors of years.
> Such multitudes I'd like to see,
> Stand free with them on free foundations.
> And then I might yet tell the moment:
> Oh stay, you are so fair!
> Then aeons could not sweep away
> The footprints of my earthly day.
> In a dream of noble rapture
> I now enjoy the highest moment.

The simultaneous grasp of the beginning and end is Faust's alpha and omega, his unholy grail of transcendence. The eternal moment holds within its dimensionless self all the antinomies associated with its medieval counterpart. However, as Faust advances in his quest, it loses some of its absoluteness; it is scaled down as Faust's stature grows to meet it.

   While circular images are occasionally evoked among several other kinds of images in *Faust*, circles and spheres do not occupy a dominant position as in the *Divine Comedy*. Nor are Goethean poetic evocations of sphericity comparable to the rigorously geometric configurations of Dante, Bruno and Pascal. What matters to Faust is "the poodle's core," and whatever is distantly free-floating in the infinite sphere can best be encompassed in a central pinpoint of ever-presentness to which all else will be peripheral.

An increasingly relaxed posture toward absolutes is apparent not only in the *Faust* drama but also in Goethe's lyric poetry. For example, in "Dauer im Wechsel" ("Permanence in Change"), composed in 1803, the sadness in the opening lines over the fleetingness of Spring is deepened by and awareness of the passing parade of the seasons:

Dauer im Wechsel

Hielte diesen frühen Segen,
Ach, nur eine Stunde fest!
Aber vollen Blütenregen
Schüttelt schon der laue West.
Soll ich mich des Grünen freuen,
Dem ich Schatten erst verdankt'?
Bald wird Sturm auch das zerstreuen,
Wenn es falb im Herbst geschwankt.

Willst du nach den Früchten greifen,
Eilig nimm dein Teil davon!
Diese fangen an zu reifen,
Und die andern keimen schon;
Gleich mit jedem Regengusse
Ändert sich dein holdes Tal,
Ach, und in demselben Flusse
Schwimmst du nicht zum zweitenmal.

Du nun selbst! Was felsenfeste
Sich vor dir hervorgetan,
Mauern siehst du, siehst Paläste
Stets mit andern Augen an.
Weggeschwunden ist die Lippe,
Die im Kusse sonst genas,
Jener Fuß, der an der Klippe
Sich mit Gemsenfreche maß.

Jene Hand, die gern und milde
Sich bewegte wohlzutun,
Das gegliederte Gebilde,
Alles ist ein andres nun.
Und was sich an jener Stelle
Nun mit deinem Namen nennt,
Kam herbei wie eine Welle,
Und so eilt's zum Element.

Laß den Anfang mit dem Ende
Sich in eins zusammenziehn!
Schneller als die Gegenstände
Selber dich vorüberfliehn.
Danke, daß die Gunst der Musen
Unvergängliches verheißt,
Den Gehalt in deinem Busen
Und die Form in deinem Geist.

Permanence in Change

If only — oh — one single hour
Could retain this early bliss!
But even now the tepid West
Is shaking loose a rain of blossoms.
Should I enjoy the new-grown greenery
To which I owe the cooling shade?
Alas, that too must fade in autumn
And be scattered by its bluster.

If you wish to grasp the fruit,
Be not tardy, take your share.
These just now begin to ripen,
While others are well past their prime.
With every drenching thundershower
Your pristine valley is transformed;
Alas, and in the selfsame river
You will not swim a second time.

And you! What once rose up
Before you, sturdy as a boulder,
These palaces and walls
You see with different eyes each day.
That lip which bloomed beneath your kiss
Is wilted now,
And your feet will never more
Scamper goatlike over dangerous cliffs.

That busy hand which gently moved
To comfort and to please,
That articulated shape,
All is now so different.
And that which now instead of you
Will answer to your name
Has surged ashore, an ocean wave,
Quick to rejoin the elements.

> The beginning and the end —
> Oh, let them draw together into one!
> Let yourself flee faster
> Than all the things you see.
> Thank the Muses who bestow
> What will be everlasting:
> The content in your bosom
> And the form within your mind.

The central image of "Permanence in Change" appears in the last two lines of the second stanza: "Alas, and in the selfsame river/You will not swim a second time." It seems appropriate for the "classical" Goethe that it should be taken from the famous ninety-first Fragment of the pre-Socratic philosopher Heraclitus which reads: "You cannot step into the same river twice."[17]

The poem's first response to the world's impermanence is to "seize the day" while it is within reach. But this impulse brings no satisfaction, because along with the surrounding changes, the observer himself changes even while vainly attempting to hold fast to each ephemeral experience.

However, in the last stanza, the plaintiveness of the opening verses is left behind and a new confident note is sounded. With the exhortation to fuse the beginning with the end, Goethe makes an indirect allusion to the circle and to its manifold figurations of eternity. Indeed, the fifth stanza may contain the second reference to Heraclitus, specifically to Fragment 103: "In the circumference of a circle, the beginning and ending are the same."[18]

Other less abstract circular images had long been in use and had effectively symbolized the coincidence of beginnings and endings. Perhaps the best known among them is the *ouroboros*, the snake biting its own tail, an emblem which Christian writers of the fourth and fifth centuries associated with Saturn-Kronos, the time-purveying god of the pagans.[19]

And even earlier, the hieroglyphic image of a serpent devouring its tail was a commonplace and fashionable adjunct to Graeco-Roman magic. Persons afflicted with various ailments would wear gems and amulets with the *ouroboros* cut into them, confident of its curative powers.[20]

---

[17] H. Diels and W. Kranz, *Die Fragmente der Vorsokratiker*, 7th ed. (Berlin, 1951), I, p. 171.

[18] *Ibid.*, p. 174.

[19] See Erwin Panofsky, *Studies in Iconography* (New York, 1970), p. 74.

[20] Campbell Bonner, *Studies in Magic Amulets, Chiefly Graeco-Egyptian* (Ann Arbor, Mich., 1950). See for example Plates II, no. 39; VI, nos. 130, 133. The important role of the *ouroboros* in the context of the emblematic tradition has been elucidated by Liselotte Dieckman in her *Hieroglyphics: The History of a Literary Symbol* (St. Louis, 1970), pp. 48-49.

Yet while one can see the allusion to the circular symbol in the lines

> The beginning and the end —
> Oh, let them draw together into one!

Goethe does not leave it at that and moves on to conclude the poem with words of praise for the Muses because they have the power to grant "what will be everlasting." And that which lasts forever — as the poem has it — is composed of content and form. One remembers that in natural science Goethe had vainly sought to bring about an amalgam of "experience" and "idea," and that the impossibility of bringing it about had brought him to the edge of despair.[21] A poem tries to *be* what it says: a fusion of content and form, terms which are sufficiently analogous to "experience" and "idea" as to give special significance to this aspect of the relationship between Goethe's natural science and his poetry.

During the stormy and stressful early phases of the composition of *Faust*, the *Augenblick*, the transcendent paradox, could be bestowed only by God and, illicitly, by Satan. Faust's attempt to win it by direct assault produced tragedy. Only as the language through which Faust as a tragic figure lives, becomes supremely conscious of itself — as in *Faust II* and in "Permanence in Change" — does it approach a new integrity and innocence. Such language will always strive to be absolutely particular and temporal, as well as absolutely universal and timeless. In this it must fail, but the quality of the attempt as well as the majesty of the failure are important aspects of the work's stature.

---

[21] See p. 69 above.

Chapter Five

VIRGINIA WOOLF:
WRESTLING WITH CHAOS

> I need a language such as lovers use, words of one syllable
> such as children speak. . . I have done with phrases.
> VIRGINIA WOOLF, *THE WAVES*

Our attention will not now be directed to a single, monumental work
as it was in the previous two chapters, and as it will be again when we
deal with a single work by Thomas Mann. Instead we will touch on
three or four of Virginia Woolf's novels, to develop a sense of how this
author, in the fullness of her great narrative powers, conveyed her anxiety about the inadequacy — at least for the life of the spirit — of the
chronological segmentation of experience.
   To be sure, none of Woolf's works has the stature, or has had the
impact of the other monumental works chosen for this investigation;
nor does one particular novel of hers as yet stand out as her one most
important book. Yet there is no denying that throughout her maturity
as a writer she experimented in significant ways with fictional time, and
especially with moments which are experienced as existing beyond the
clocks and calendars of our daily existence.
   We will therefore present to our mind's eye differing moments from
several of Woolf's narrative works in order to follow the manifestations
of a single overriding problem which haunted a great writer to the point
of obsession.
   Down to Virginia Woolf's last novel, an underlying formlessness can
be felt even through the most exquisitely wrought artifice of her prose.
Tremors from this precarious condition are present already in such a
very early work as *Night and Day* (1919). Here is how she wrote about

the heroine as she ambles through Kew Gardens on the first warm day of Spring, in the company of her knowledgeable friend Ralph Denham

> [Katherine Hilbery] wished he could go on forever talking of plants, and showing her how science felt not quite blindly for the law that ruled their endless variations. A law that might be inscrutable but was certainly omnipotent appealed to her at the moment, because she could find nothing like it in possession of human lives. (p. 331)

Even when Woolf came closest to achieving an almost seamlessly unified lyrical composition, as in *The Waves* (1931), the final monologue of Bernard, the "maker of phrases," provides a glimpse of the chaos beneath the managed and choreographed forms of human life:

> . . . one girl on a bicycle who, as she rode, seemed to lift the corner of a curtain concealing the populous, undifferentiated chaos of life which surged behind the outlines of my friends and the willow tree. (p. 177)

And in her last novel, *Between the Acts* (1941), written not long before her death, a disembodied voice issues from a loudspeaker hidden behind a clump of shrubbery:

> Look at yourselves, ladies and gentlemen! Then at the wall; and ask how's this wall, the great wall, which we call, perhaps miscall, civilisation, to be built by . . . orts, scraps and fragments like ourselves. (p. 108)

Traditional systems and conventions were painfully irrelevant to Woolf, who had doubts even about the existence of an individual self which in novels such as *Mrs. Dalloway* (1925), and at its purest in *The Waves*, rises to the surface through a welter of competing impressions. The self becomes manifest not as a delimited spiritual entity but — as in Jean Guiguet's phrase — a "potential of relations."[1] But surely the most telling commentary on this important feature of the writer's philosophic and narrative stance came from herself, when she said in her essay, "Modern Fiction," written in 1925, the year during which *Mrs. Dalloway* was completed:

> . . . if the writer could base his work upon his own feeling and not upon convention, there would be no plot, no comedy, no tragedy, no love interest or catastrophe in the accepted style, and perhaps not a single button sewn on as the Bond Street tailors would have it.[2]

Such a position tends to push the rationale which sustains literary creation close to its pre-lingual source. It was not the norm among 19th and early 20th-century novelists to pull the rug out from under the

---

[1] Jean Guiguet, *Virginia Woolf and Her Works* (New York: Harcourt, 1965), p. 36.
[2] *The Common Reader* (London: The Hogarth Press, 1925), p. 189.

own enterprise. Charles Dickens, George Eliot, and Tolstoy were still writing in a tradition which, generally speaking, showed confidence in the efficacy and reliability of words and phrases. The abyss began to open for the generation of writers and thinkers who reached maturity during the first third of this century. The dividing line can by no means be neatly drawn. There were the 19th-century precursors of the modern consciousness like Kierkegaard, Nietzsche and Bergson, and there were those who, though born later, were content in some or all of their works to expand the compass and deepen the roots of nineteenth-century conventions, like Thomas Mann in *Buddenbrooks* (1901), Galsworthy in the *Forsyte Saga* series (1906-1920), and E.M. Forster in *A Passage to India* (1924).

The revaluation of the nature of matter and energy resulting from the consequences of Max Planck's quantum theory, the new conceptions of time and space being developed under the impact of Einstein's special and general theories of relativity — these were but two markers pointing toward unexplored regions. When Arthur Eddington actually observed and measured the bending of starlight by the gravitational field of the sun, thereby confirming Einstein's calculations, the name of Einstein became a household word throughout Europe. Planck's revolutionary perspective on the nature of energy became a factor in European culture at about the same time. Einstein and Planck were only the most eminent among scientists who provided the impetus for new modes of thought and quite unpredictable new art forms.[3] If one adds to the revolution in physics the reluctant though widespread acceptance, beginning about 1915, of Freud's theories of the operations of the unconscious mind, then it is not difficult to see that revolutionary developments in the natural and humane sciences were bound to permeate all intellectual and artistic endeavors. A reorientation of fictive perspectives that would reflect the new sensibility had become a matter of artistic integrity and viability.

Virginia Woolf, along with other members of the Bloomsbury group, was alive to the tremors reaching her from the Continent and from contemporary English writers. No doubt Woolf absorbed into her own sensorium Bergson's distinction between chronological time and experienced duration; one can clearly discern how she made this distinction a kind of trademark, yet one must also acknowledge that she did so while being essentially quite faithful to traditional modes. This distinguishes her from iconoclasts like Samuel Beckett and Ionesco, Apollinaire of the *"Epigrammes,"* and Alain Robbe-Grillet, the creator of the

---

[3] There is a brief but excellent account of the impact of science on literature during the first third of the twentieth century in Theodore Ziolkowski's *The Novels of Hermann Hesse* (Princeton, N.J.: Princeton University Press, 1965), pp. 16-18.

"*nouveau roman.*" Woolf's fictions have beginnings, middles and endings. Even in "The Mark on the Wall" the plot moves from "now" to "later" to "last"; one progresses from the "Perhaps it was the middle of January . . ." to "I must jump up and see for myself . . ." at the turning point, to "Ah, the mark on the wall! It was a snail," the last line of the nine-page story signaling a return to the beginning. Nor does a novel like *Mrs. Dalloway* leave any doubt concerning the time and place of the action. It opens with a morning's shopping trip in the middle of June soon after World War I and it ends with the departure of Clarissa's guests after one of her notable parties. In novels like *To the Lighthouse* (1927) and the fictional biography *Orlando* (1928), and even in the most lyrical of her novels, *The Waves* (1931), the author provided sufficient spatial and temporal markers to orient the reader. It is time which constitutes both the true subject and the underlying structure of most of Virginia Woolf's works of fiction. Most of her book titles direct readers to this predominant concern: *Night and Day* (1919), *Monday or Tuesday* (1921), *The Hours* (the original title of *Mrs. Dalloway*), *The Years* (1937), *Between the Acts* (1941). Even *The Waves* could be included in this list, if one thinks of waves as a metaphor for the pulse and flow of time. We will glance at Woolf's narrative works between 1925 and 1941 — from *Mrs. Dalloway* to *Between the Acts* — and seek ways of dealing with certain aspects of her art which, in full admiration, will have to be looked upon as one of literature's glorious defeats in the face of insuperable odds.

We know from Woolf's diary that she read Joyce's *Portrait of the Artist* in 1919 and *Ulysses* in 1922, and that it was only *after* the experience of Joyce that she embarked on Proust's *A la recherche du temps perdu*. Her estimate of Joyce ranged from ambivalence to hostility. She declared the cemetery scene in *Ulysses* a masterpiece, only to undercut her initial praise with a set of hostile questions:

> Is it Joyce's method that inhibits the creative power? Is it due to the method that we feel neither jovial nor magnanimous, but centred in a self which, in spite of its tremors of susceptibility, never embraces or creates what is outside itself and beyond? Does the emphasis laid perhaps didactically, upon indecency, contribute to the effect of something angular and isolated?[4]

It became obvious that there was a clash between incompatible temperaments, between two writers who yet appeared to move toward similar goals as writers of fiction. Regarding her own narrative experiments, the short stories "The Mark on the Wall" and "An Unwritten Novel," she noted on January 26, 1920: "I suppose the danger is the damned

---

[4] *The Common Reader*, p. 191.

egotistical self; which ruins Joyce and [Dorothy] Richardson to my mind: is one pliant and rich enough to provide a wall for the book from oneself without its becoming, as in Joyce and Richardson, narrowing and restricting?"⁵

Her reading of Proust, on the other hand, was an unequivocally joyful experience. She was forty years old when she wrote on October 3, 1922 to her friend Roger Fry how Proust, even in translation, was like a revelation to her: "I am in a state of amazement, as if a miracle were being performed before my eyes. How, at last, has someone solidified what has always escaped — and made it too into this beautiful and perfectly enduring substance?"⁶ Here there is none of the *animus* which she harbored against Joyce. In Proust she admired a kindred soul. His probings into time and "involuntary" memory, his mastery of the seemingly trivial detail, these were also near the center of Virginia Woolf's concerns. In her own fictions, however, her reading experiences became integral parts of new, immensely complex and peculiarly Woolfian patterns. After all, "The Mark on the Wall" and "An Unwritten Novel" were fully as "Proustian" as *Mrs. Dalloway*, and they were published in 1921 before she had read any Proust at all.

While composing *The Hours*, later to be called *Mrs. Dalloway*, she was freshly emerging from her reading of Proust, and yet in her diary she did not relate herself to him. Instead she invoked Dostoevski, deploring her own intellectualism and admitting to a sense of insecurity as a writer when comparing her verbal explorations of subtle shifts in perception to the cathartic passions of Dostoevskian characters. On June 19, 1923, she confided to her diary: "One must write from deep feeling, said Dostoevski. And do I? Or do I fabricate with words, loving them as I do?"⁷ Perhaps she was only dimly aware of the distant ideal of a new kind of novel. At times she was troubled by her own compulsion to strip language of the kind of concreteness and particularity which she savored and applauded in the prose of other writers. In moments of self-doubt she questioned her ability to convey reality with sufficient conviction:

> I daresay it's true, however, that I haven't that "reality" gift. I insubstandise, wilfully to some extent, distrusting reality — its cheapness. . . Have I the power of conveying the true reality? Or do I write essays about myself?⁸

She was groping, it appears, for a primordial state of the spirit in which spatial and temporal perceptions could be experienced, as it were, for

---

⁵ *A Writer's Diary* (New York, 1973), p. 22.
⁶ *The Letters of Virginia Woolf*, ed. Nigel Nicolson (New York, 1976), p. 566.
⁷ *A Writer's Diary*, p. 56.
⁸ *Ibid.*

the first time. As she envisaged this state, its very radiance sometimes made her wish to shun ready-made linguistic and cultural conventions in favor of the immediacy of formless mutterings. Near the end of *The Waves* we read:

> What is the phrase for the moon? And the phrase for love? By what name are we to call death? I do not know. I need a little language such as lovers use, words of one syllable such as children speak. . . . I need a howl; a cry. When the storm crosses the marsh and sweeps over me where I lie in ,the ditch unregarded I need no words. Nothing neat. None of those resonances and lovely echoes that break and chime from nerve to nerve in our breasts, making wild music, false phrases. I have done with phrases. (p. 209)

The paradox in this remarkable passage is obvious. A liberation *from* language must come *through* language. This is as true of her most verbally adept character, Bernard, as it is for Virginia Woolf herself. As readers we witness the stratagems and gestures which she employed in order to extricate words and phrases from a maze of indirections and to make them into windows of unmediated experience.

Outside of language there would be no classes of objects and no preordained systems of value. In this imagined state of innocence, the author devoutly opened herself to *all* kinds of impressions and made a resolute attempt to prejudge nothing. At the time of writing *Mrs. Dalloway*, Woolf offered this reflection:

> The mind receives a myriad impressions — trivial, fantastic, evanescent, or engraved with the sharpness of steel. From all sides they come, an incessant shower of innumerable atoms; and as they fall, as they shape themselves into the life of Monday or Tuesday, the accent falls differently from of old; the moment of importance came not here but there. . . .[9]

She was driven, without recourse, into a radical authenticity, toward a zero level where she was open to multitudinous unrelated stimuli. And yet coherences inevitably emerged, and clusters of perceptions acquired meaning and value. In the course of the creative process, she submitted herself to the discipline of articulate discourse and to the conventions of storytelling. And indeed, Virginia Woolf loved words — perhaps too much so, she thought — and devised exquisite verbal constructs which sometimes give the impression of being overly delicate and too precariously balanced.

Woolf puts into question her own linguistic and narrative devices which imperiously mark the progress of the hours in *Mrs. Dalloway*. The clocks of London's Harley Street "nibble at the June day . . .

---

[9] *The Common Reader, op. cit.,* p. 189.

shredding and slicing, dividing and subdividing," and neither Clarissa Dalloway nor Peter Walsh nor Septimus Smith are inwardly in step with clocks and calendars. Their lives are a series of discrete moments which, when destiny or chance conspires to bring about their felicitous conjunction, will free them from the prisonhouse of one-thing-after-anotherness, of a dreary and repetitive Monday-through-Sunday routine, allowing them to experience life as a single and undiluted essence. Nowhere more persistently than in *Mrs. Dalloway* did the author dwell on the disparity between chronology and experienced duration: the former, a fundamental condition for civilized and regulated living, the other, the direct experience of time, useless for all practical purposes, but gloriously beyond the pale of calendars and clocks. Early in the novel, Clarissa muses about an event some thirty years in the past: then, for that moment, she had an illumination; "a match burning in a crocus; an inner meaning almost expressed" (p. 47). Clarissa is fifty-two at the time of this recollection; her "moment" had occurred many years earlier: the astonished recognition of an erotic bond between herself and her friend Sally Seton when both were very young. The experience now reshapes itself as a memory embedded in the narrative's present time — a brief respite from the preparations for the evening's important party. The past becomes present as the events begin to coalesce during "the moment of this June morning on which was the pressure of all the other mornings . . . collecting the whole of her at one point (as she looked into the glass)" (p. 54). But Clarissa must give heed to the "leaden circles of sound" emanating from Big Ben and to methodical professionals like Dr. Bradshaw, the prominent London physician who manages mental cases with quiet authority and disastrously irrelevant common sense. His patient, Septimus Smith, fresh out of the trenches of the first World War, is stubbornly slipping into insanity. He gradually removes himself from Big Ben and the quotidian chores and fixes his unhinged mind on the one revelatory moment that might bring meaning into his life. The "sane" Clarissa has become an admiring disciple of Septimus Smith. In her mind, his suicide becomes a fanfare of integrity. The narrator's own voice allows the reader to participate in a moment of special luminosity:

> A thing there was that mattered; a thing wreathed about this chatter, defaced, obscured in her own life, let drop every day in corruption, lies, chatter. This Septimus had preserved. Death was defiance. Death was an attempt to communicate; people feeling the impossibility of reaching the centre which, mystically, evaded them; closeness drew apart; rapture faded, one was alone. There was an embrace in death. (pp. 280-281)

The narrator's voice that could also be Clarissa's continues: ". . . had he plunged holding his treasure?" The answer is unknowable to Clarissa and to us, but its allure and paradoxical potential are upheld to the end of the novel, for Septimus Smith had gained access to an "idiotic" — or highly special — vision of "the center." Because he was mad, his epiphany was self-invalidating and tantamount to a spiritual short circuit. For Virginia Woolf, as well as for this memorable character, the center, or sufficient moment, was a goal dimly envisioned from the outermost verge of human reach.

In some ways, *To the Lighthouse* is a more artfully constructed novel than *Mrs. Dalloway*. It consists of two distinct plots, separated not by their locale but by the passage of ten years. The earlier unit is dominated by the presence of Mrs. Ramsay, who sets the tone of the family's seaside vacation home on an island in the Hebrides. In the second and final section of the book, Lily Briscoe has moved center stage. Mrs. Ramsay had died at the end of the first part, and what had been promised to two of the Ramsay children when they were six and seven in part one — a day-long trip to the lighthouse in the company of their father, Professor Ramsay — is belatedly fulfilled for the now teen-age youngsters. With apparent irony, the pivotal events in time are mentioned in parentheses, as if of no importance, while actually chronicity has a tyrannical grip on events and is in no danger of losing its quite unparenthetical control: "(Mrs. Ramsay dies)," "(the Ramsays's son Andrew is killed by a shell in the trenches in France)," "(the daughter Prue dies in childbirth)", "(Lily Briscoe arrives at the Ramsay vacation house after an absence of ten years)" — all these punctuate the progression of the novel's plot, and in that sense they are central rather than peripheral. The parentheses therefore are ironic in the sense that they enclose quite unparenthetical matters; it is like calling a fat person "skinny" and a tall one "shorty." In this instance, however, it turns out that to regard the parentheses as ironic and therefore untrustworthy would be missing the point, because temporal events when seen *sub specie aeternitatis* are indeed adventitious, parenthetical and almost ludricrously insignificant aspects of a central and timeless truth. The parentheses have a double bottom and in their tricky way can transmit the metaphysical situation truthfully and unironically. Characteristically, Woolf devises ever new ways of bringing about a confrontation between traditional temporal habits and an encompassing present moment.

An eminent academic philosopher, Mr. Ramsay in *To the Lighthouse* forges his way from problem to problem, never proceeding until the thicket before him has been cleared. The narrator offers this characterization:

> For if thought is like the keyboard of a piano, divided into many notes, or
> like the alphabet is ranged in twenty-six letters all in order, then this splendid

mind had no sort of difficulty in running over those letters one by one, firmly and accurately, until it had reached, say, the letter Q. He reached Q. (p. 53)

With his tenacious advance to the seventeenth letter of the alphabet, Mr. Ramsay had reached the frontier of his great intellect. After Q there was darkness. The narrator divides humanity into two categories:

> . . . on the one hand [there are] the steady goers of superhuman strength who, plodding and persevering, repeat the whole alphabet in order, twenty-six letters in all, from start to finish, on the other the gifted, the inspired who, miraculously, lump all the letters together in one flash — the way of genius. (p. 55)

a position which perhaps marks the distinction between artistic and scholarly temperaments.

Miss Briscoe, a friend of the family, is a painter. In the first section of *To the Lighthouse* she had attempted to imbue her brush strokes with direction and purpose — to no avail. The painting would lack a "center" until the plot was completed in the third and last part of the novel. Finally, as the boat sails to the lighthouse, Lily Briscoe is able to "tunnel her way into the picture" (p. 258) in order to bring the past into the presentness of her canvas, *our* canvas, or the novel which we are reading. As Lily Briscoe sits on the lawn, brush in hand before her easel, she has a view of the ocean and the lighthouse in the distance. Mr. Carmichael, the aged poet of no great significance, lies snoozing nearby on his deckchair. The narrator gives an account of Lily's thoughts:

> But one only awoke people if one knew what one wanted to say to them. And she wanted to say not one thing, but everything. Little words that broke up the thought and dismembered it said nothing. 'About life, about death; about Mrs. Ramsay.' (p. 265)

But saying "everything" takes time and takes space. That is man's frustration, and a novelist's challenge which can never be entirely met. Images and structural devices may carry a powerful allusive charge and launch the reader toward an intimation of simultaneity, but the mystical experience as such cannot be transcribed because, for one thing, it contradicts the temporal nature of language. The all-at-once experience is irrational and can be approached only by way of a religious or artistic vision. *To the Lighthouse* ends thus:

> Lily Briscoe looked at her canvas; it was blurred. With a sudden intensity, as if she saw it clear for a second, she drew a line there, in the centre. It was done; it was finished. Yes, she thought, laying down her brush in extreme fatigue, I have had my vision. (p. 310)

The "centre" of Lily Briscoe's painting cannot be determined by reference to physical coordinates, nor is it a marker along a line of successive events, even though it shares some characteristics with both. It is a privileged and encompassing spatio-temporal pinpoint, one among many variants. But it is not a moment that belongs entirely to Lily Briscoe. She is the instrument, the "tunnelling" aesthetic consciousness by which the numerous strands of the novel — pictorially transmuted on the canvas — are gathered into irreducible meaning. Here the chronology of the plot appears fused in a focal point of simultaneity. True, by finding the aesthetic center, Miss Briscoe serves the novel more than herself. She does not leave us persuaded that her seascape has the grandeur of an epocal painting, nor that she herself — as a result of her inspired aesthetic solution — will henceforth have the stature of a major artist. The importance of Miss Briscoe's liberating insight lies rather in the power of her new-found center to contain, and give meaning to, the disparate elements of the life that had surged about her.

In *The Waves*, a novel which traces the lives of six friends from childhood to maturity, verbal exchanges between members of this close-knit group unobtrusively mark the progression of time. Yet the characters are not discoursing in any realistic or recognizably dramatic manner. Their verbalizations amount to fragmentary observations, arranged in ostensibly non-casual sequences. Voices without personal inflections issue either from Bernard, Louis, and Neville — or else from Susan, Rhoda and Jinny. A distilled impersonal speech dominates much of the novel, and each of the characters has accommodated him- or herself to his or her own abstraction. The opening lines of the novel set the tone:

> "I see a ring," said Bernard, "hanging above me. It quivers and hangs in a loop of light."
> "I see a slab of pale yellow," said Susan, "spreading away until it meets a purple stripe."
> "I hear a sound," said Rhoda, "cheep, chirp; cheep, chirp; going up and down."
> "I see a crimson tassel," said Jinny, "twisted, with gold threads."

And so it continues over more than two pages. To be sure, these are children's voices, but the absence of any personal inflections or speech patterns, the willfully undifferentiated uses of "I see" and "I hear" spilling over from a general reservoir of human speech, the fragmentary sensations, recorded seemingly at random, all these indicate a departure from novelistic convention and a groping toward a narrative mode in keeping with a nascent modern sensibility. This new and experimental manner is also a natural consequence of Woolf's declaration of intent concerning *The Waves*, as noted in her diary:

> The idea has come to me that what I want now to do is to saturate every atom

. . . give the moment whole; whatever it includes . . . I want to put practically everything in: yet to saturate. That is what I want to do in *The Moths*.¹⁰ It must include nonsense, fact, sordidity: but made transparent. (*A Writer's Diary*, p. 136)

It is only rarely that Woolf's "atoms," in a vertiginous moment of heightened consciousness, organize themselves into clusters in which fact and meaning are fused in a seamless union. It is Bernard who seeks to convey such a moment in this final summing up of the lives of six friends, including his own; six lives, distinct and individual by nature, yet each made an inseparable part of a larger unit by the common experience of friendship, love and hate:

. . . here we were; I in my serge suit; she Jinny in green. There was no past, no future; merely the moment in its ring of light, and our bodies; and the inevitable climax, the ecstasy. (p. 179)

The time span represented in Woolf's novels has no essential bearing on the evocation of those epiphanic moments when sequential events coalesce into irreducible points of self-evident meaning. *Mrs. Dalloway* and *Between the Acts* take place in a single day; a number of years are traversed in *To the Lighthouse* and *The Waves*, while Orlando blithely moves from boyhood to adulthood through five centuries of British history, from Elizabethan times to 1928, the year of the biography's composition. In Orlando's new feminine incarnation, "she" glances with instant understanding at the poem entitled "Oak Tree," which (near the beginning of the novel) had been written in "her own boyish hand," and marvels at the fact that she had been working at the poem "for close on three hundred years" (p. 236).

Seconds of daydreaming can evoke aeons in the evolution of life on earth, as they do for Mrs. Swithin in *Between the Acts*, while she pores over her favorite book, *An Outline of History*:

. . . [she] had spent the hours . . . thinking of rhododendron forests in Piccadilly; when the entire continent, not then, she understood, divided by a channel, was all one; populated, she understood, by elephant-bodied, seal-necked, heaving, surging, slowly writhing and, she supposed, barking monsters. . . . It took her five seconds in actual time, in mind time ever so much longer. . . . she was given to increasing the bounds of the moment by flights into the past or future. (pp. 8-9)

And in narratives whose plots extend horizontally over several years, memory and expectation are in the end compressed into a kind of vertical chord. Bernard in *The Waves* succeeds in articulating such privileged simultaneity in exemplary fashion:

---

¹⁰ The original working title of *The Waves*.

. . . we six, out of how many million millions, for one moment out of what measureless abundance of past time and time to come, burnt there triumphant. The moment was all; the moment was enough. (p. 197)

The ticking of clocks, the chiming of Big Ben, the progression of weeks and years are given their full linear sway in Woolf's novels, but at culminating moments there occurs a liberation from the stranglehold of time, along with the enactment of a transcendent reintegration in a non-dimensional point. To be sure, as soon as the last page has been turned, such a verbal victory over time is bound to be revealed as pyrrhic, but in the arena of poetry, none more glorious comes to mind.

Though confident in her narrative powers — certainly after the critical success of *Mrs. Dalloway* in 1925 — Woolf also had a strong anti-substantiating bent which informed and sometimes dominated her writings, with the result that often the reader is forced to deal with vague impressions and is given but few particulars on which to fasten his imagination. Clarissa Dalloway reaches us through her spiritual essence and not really by a palpable presence that might function as a correlative to her character. As a highly esteemed hostess "she stands at the top of the stairs" in the Dalloways' London house. The image is at first evoked by Clarissa herself as she recalls a phrase that had once been used scoldingly by Peter Walsh, whom she had almost married many years ago, before he went off to India. And it crops up again in her mind later in the book, this time in a context of vague yearning and emotional discomfort. As a lady surveying the scene from the top of the stairway Clarissa effectively symbolizes her role in London society. In so far as the phrase appears only in connection with Peter Walsh, it brings home the melancholy of a middle-aged woman who can no longer follow deliciously reckless impulses. But she is too complex, or perhaps too undefined a personality, to be either "this or that" entity drawn from the reservoir of human possibilities. Woolf's fondness for these demonsrtative pronouns — "this" and "that" — is evident in her fiction[11] as well as in her diary.

. . . a thing I see before me: something abstract; but residing in the downs or sky; beside which nothing matters; in which I shall rest and continue to exist! Reality I call it. And I fancy sometimes this is the most necessary thing to me: that which I seek. But who knows — once one takes a pen and writes? How difficult not to go on making "reality" this and that, whereas it is one thing. . . .[12]

On the first page of *To the Lighthouse*, the author gives us a glimpse of Mr. Ramsay through the eyes of his six-year-old son James. There

[11] ". . . and she would not say of Peter, she would not say of herself, I am this, am that" (*Mrs. Dalloway*, p. 11).
[12] *A Writer's Diary*, pp. 129-130.

would be no trip to the lighthouse the following day, a disappointing
bit of news for the boy who had been looking forward to the exciting
boat ride:

> What [James' father] said was true. It was always true. He was incapable of
> untruth; never tampered with a fact; never altered a disagreeable word to suit
> the pleasure or convenience of any mortal being, least of all his own chil-
> dren. . . . (pp. 10-11)

Here as elsewhere, the author has created a presence. We feel it through
the effect Mr. Ramsay has on those with whom he comes into contact:
his wife, his disciples, his friends. This manner of conjuring up an
essential individual self in the form of a "luminous halo" is inseparable
from other important aspects of Woolf's narrative art, and it is in conformity with her spiritual and philosophic anxieties regarding the very
possibility of a "self," and her doubts with regard to any meaningful
coherences between "scraps, orts and fragments."[13] A radical and tenacious honesty is required to uphold such a perilous situation at the frontier of nihilism. The atoms or scraps impinging on the senses remain
stubbornly separate, in spite of what language can do to force them into
the larger confederacies about whose name a consensus may or may not
develop.

If Virginia Woolf found it difficult to come to terms with a conceptual
definition of the Self, and resorted to the image of an aura of light in
order to convey the presence of an important character, then it must
have been a correspondingly even more arduous task to make sense of
fragmentary events that are free-floating in time and space. "Making
sense" after all involves naming and attending to those privileged
moments in which meanings emerge from surrounding chaos. In defer-
ence to such moments it would be insensitive to the point of callousness
if the characters were shown plodding through the day "from breakfast
to lunch" and onward, and enforcing their fictive existence mainly by
dint of outward appearance and behavior. Woolf's particular narrative
stance first appears as a bold experiment in "The Mark on the Wall,"
written about 1920, and was never abandoned:

> As we face each other in omnibuses and underground railways we are looking
> into the mirror; that accounts for the vagueness, the gleam of glassiness, in
> our eyes. And the novelists in future will realize more and more the impor-
> tance of these reflections, for of course there is not one reflection but an almost
> infinite number; those are the depths they will explore, those the phantoms
> they will pursue, leaving the description of reality more and more out of their

---

[13] Note the frequent invocation of these words in *Between the Acts* (for example, pp.
188, 189, 215). See also p. 86 above.

stories, taking a knowledge of it for granted, as did the Greeks and Shakespeare perhaps — but these generalizations are very worthless. The military sound of the word is enough. It recalls leading articles, cabinet ministers — a whole class of things indeed which, as a child, one thought as the thing itself, the standard thing, the real thing, from which we could not depart save at the risk of nameless damnation. (p. 41)

That passage might well serve to illuminate Woolf's chief concerns as a novelist. It rings true not only for the story of which it is a part, but may be applied with equal justice to the final two decades of her life. Her last novel, *Between the Acts*, is made of the same spiritual fabric and is different only by virtue of its greatly heightened compositional scope and structural boldness. Pointz Hall, a country house and social center, is the sole scene of action. Old Mrs. Swithin, the owner's widowed sister-in-law is a summer guest. Reflecting on the pageant of English history that had just been performed on an outdoor makeshift stage erected on the grounds of Pointz Hall, she and young Isa have this exchange:

> "This year, last year, next year, never . . ." Isa murmured. Her hand burnt in the sun on the window sill. Mrs. Swithin took the knitting from the table.
> "Did you feel," Mrs. Swithin asked, "what he said: we act different parts but are the same?"
> "Yes," Isa answered, "No," she added. It was Yes, No. Yes, yes, yes, the tide rushed out embracing. No, no, it contracted. . . .
> "Orts, scraps and fragments," she quoted what she remembered of the vanishing play. (p. 215)

These words would not be out of place as a commentary on, say, the six friends in *The Waves*. They lead separate lives, and yet there is about them a unity which, in an important sense, makes them a single entity.

Images of centrality may arise in Woolf's fiction whenever a chaos of sense impressions is marshaled into communicable meaning, as when Bernard, in his "summing up" near the end of *The Waves* says: "Let us again pretend that life is a solid substance, shaped like a globe, which we turn about in our fingers" (p. 178). And a bit later, as though finding fault with the "solid" substance and as though attempting to bring it closer to the author's more familiar image of an "aura," or a "luminous halo," she has Bernard say: "The crystal, the globe of life as one calls it, far from being hard and cold to the touch, has walls of thinnest air" (p. 182). Earlier in the same novel, Bernard had already expanded "the globe" to infinite magnitude in a way which to a receptive mind might seem close to a religious meditation:

> Yet there are moments when the walls of the mind grow thin; when nothing is unabsorbed, and I could fancy that we might blow so vast a bubble that

the sun might set and rise in it and we might take the blue of midday and the black of midnight and be cast off and escape from the here and now. (p. 159)

Similar intimations of cosmic sphericity are not difficult to find in *Mrs. Dalloway, Orlando,* and the other late novels. Invariably the circle or sphere evokes expectations of a center. However, equally important as the images created by words and phrases are the structural aspects of the text as a whole. In *To the Lighthouse,* as we discussed earlier, Lily Briscoe is first seen at her easel, staring at the canvas and unable to break through to a meaningful pictorial form, and in the end she is shown in exactly the same position. This time she can complete the picture with confidence. Because the circle of the fiction has now been completed, she is able to find the center as if by a divining rod.

The need to confront a whirlpool of impressions without the protective armor of convention and to forge coherences without prior commitments, is at the heart of Woolf's endeavors. In the novels of such Edwardian authors as H.G. Wells, Galsworthy and Arnold Bennett, whose fictional modes Woolf sternly rejected, the links between language and reality, between outward movement and internal energies, were solid and remained essentially unquestioned. The contradictory impulses of the human psyche had not yet moved center-stage, and consequently the personages in their fictions were either "this" or "that," as Virginia Woolf might have said. They would act in a manner all too consistent with their discernible attributes.[14] Woolf's ostensible plots are peripheral. The true locale of dramatic and sometimes desperate action is the caves and tunnels of the mind whose inner processes constitute the subject of her novels. These processes integrate — or fail to integrate — the scraps, orts and fragments into namable phenomena.

The object of Virginia Woolf's perennially hopeless quest is not the periphery but the center. Because it is as small as the imagination can make it, and because it encompasses as much world as is conceivable, the "point" must be seen as the ultimate paradox, much like Pascal's innermost sphere or Blake's "world in a grain of sand." In at least one phase of her creative life, Woolf sought access to it by means of simple, short words cast adrift as it were, and meaning nothing in particular and everything in general. As Bernard says in *The Waves:*

---

[14] This is how Mrs. Woolf phrased the matter in her essay "Modern Fiction": "Whether we call it life or spirit, truth or reality, this, the essential thing, has moved off, or on, and refuses to be contained any longer in such ill-fitting vestments as we provide" (*The Common Reader,* p. 188).

> How tired I am of stories, how tired I am of phrases that come down beautifully with all their feet on the ground. . . . I begin to long for some little language such as lovers use, broken words, like the shuffling of their feet on the pavement. (p. 169)

and again close to the end of the novel:

> I need a little language such as lovers use, words of one syllable such as children speak when they come into the room and find their mother sewing. (p. 209)

This is how the author registered her disenchantment with what made her into a writer: her talent and consummate artistry. In the face of what she had sought — a single, unified and unmediated vision — all her great resources had not sufficed. Surely it took courage to move open-eyed toward the abyss.

So intimately entwined are Virginia Woolf's life and art that often one seems merely to confirm the other. For example, in the memoir "Moments of Being," almost certainly jotted down without intent of publication, she seems at pains to provide a factual account — by way of a rigorous self-examination — of the manner in which she came to experience time, and what such experience had come to mean to her work. We thus learn of the biographical basis for her abiding quest — through the entire range of her mature fiction — for those singular moments which somehow hover enticingly above the repetitive patterns of daily life. Only at such junctures in her life, she explains, when she had been raised to the highest level of consciousness, did she consider herself as "existing" in the full sense of the word.

> What then has remained interesting? Again those moments of being. Two I always remember. There was the moment of the puddle in the path; when for no reason I could discover, everything suddenly became unreal; I was suspended; I could not step across the puddle; I tried to touch something . . . the whole world became unreal. Next, the other moment when the idiot boy spring up with his hand outstretched mewing, slit-eyed, red-rimmed; and without saying a word, with a sense of horror in me, I poured into his hand a bag of Russian toffee. But it was not over, for that night in the bath the dumb horror came over me. Again I had that hopeless sadness; that collapse I had described before; as if I were passive under some sledgehammer blow; exposed to a whole avalanche of meaning that had heaped itself up and dis-

charged itself upon me, unprotected, with nothing to ward it off, so that I huddled up at my end of the bath, motionless. I could not explain it; I said nothing even to Nessa sponging herself at the other end.[15]

Because we live most of our lives in a state of partial or obscure awareness, our "moments of being" are infrequent, isolated, or kept at a safe distance, embedded as we are in the "cotton wool" of our habitual daily rhythms. Yet outside of such moments there is no "being." The relative pleasantness or misery of such moments is not at issue; they can be either. What matters is that they be fully meaningful and fully factual, that is fully universal and fully particular. They must happen at a particular time in order to happen at all times.

---

[15] *Virginia Woolf, Moments of Being,* ed. Jeanne Schulkind (New York, London: Harcourt, 1976), p. 78.

Chapter Six

THOMAS MANN'S *DOCTOR FAUSTUS*: BREAKTHROUGH TO THE VERTICAL CHORD

> A work of art is always conceived of as a single whole, and even though according to aesthetic philosophy a work of verbal and musical art — as distinct from one in the visual arts — is necessarily temporal and sequential in nature, it yet strives to be completely *there* at every moment.
>
> THOMAS MANN, *DIE ENTSTEHUNG DES DOKTOR FAUSTUS*

Mann's *Faustus* is one among a few great novels of the twentieth century which usher in an important phase — perhaps a final phase — in a long-standing quest for poetically imaged simultaneity. The book is the arena for a struggle between language as a temporal phenomenon on the one hand, and the non-temporal meanings signified, or alluded to, on the other — a struggle engaged in against impossible odds, in order to bring about a merging of antithetical and mutually exclusive categories of perception. The fusion of time and non-time into a "concretely universal" presentness can therefore be seen as the goal obsessively sought by the novel's hero. He alone must accept the disastrous consequences of his commitment to the "breakthrough" into a region of absolute creativity. Adrian Leverkühn lives his life under the aegis of a single, overpowering quest which leaves nothing that it touches unaffected. Even Serenus Zeitblom, Adrian's friend and fictive biographer, is not immune to it, though his profession — classical philology — and indeed his very name, evoke an identification with the temporal nature of life. Zeitblom becomes restless when faced with the necessity of setting down his friend's life as a succession of events:

> Ah, I write badly! My greed for saying everything at once makes my sentences overflow their banks, drives them away from the thought which they had set out to record. . . .[1]

For Adrian, on the other hand, events in time, such as the sounding of musical notes, are merely the raw material to be molded into a new structure of comprehensive simultaneity. Chronological or horizontal sequences are secondary manifestations of more significant "all-at-once" complexes. Even as a pupil in elementary school, when Adrian's affinity to music became apparent, he was attracted to the possibility of converting a horizontal tonal row into its vertical equivalent. Serenus Zeitblom records:

> In the school yard . . . he would speak to me about such magical diversions of his idle hours: the transformation, with which he was above all preoccupied, of the interval into the chord, of the horizontal into the vertical, of the successive into the simultaneous. Simultaneity, he asserted, was of primary concern in this process, for even the single note, with its near and more distant overtones, constitutes a chord, and the musical scale was only an analytical unfolding of the chord into a corresponding horizontal row.[2]

In the course of a friendship which reached back into a shared childhood, Zeitblom had become well aware of Leverkühn's genius and of his importance to the development of music. He regarded it as his duty to mankind to record his friend's life, and three years after Adrian's death, began to devote himself to this task. This "biography" is in fact the novel to which Thomas Mann gave the subtitle "The Life of the German Composer Leverkühn as Told by a Friend." Zeitblom's own feelings, which occasionally surface during his biographical labors, alternate between devoted love for a friend, reverence and awe for his genius, lingering hurt for his aloofness toward him, and remembered anxiety over his well-being. Even as a child, Adrian had shown signs — at least to Zeitblom's attentive soul — of being marked not only for greatness but also for suffering and tragedy.

When, as adults, the two friends had attained their full intellectual powers, Zeitblom had remained somewhat skeptical concerning Adrian's imperious and self-imposed demand for "strict style" (*strenger Satz*) as the basis for musical composition, and he could muster only an antiquarian's interest in an old print representing a "magic square" tacked to the wall above Adrian's upright piano. Adrian had found it in a second-hand bookshop. Actually, it was a detail based on Dürer's "Melencholia." in which the magic square, along with an hour glass, an

---

[1] Thomas Mann, *Doktor Faustus* (Frankfurt, 1960), p. 468. Hereafter cited as *D.F.* This and other translations from the German in this chapter are mine.

[2] *D.F.*, p. 101.

apothecary scale, and other allegorical objects, fill the space around a central female figure. The magic square was divided into "sixteen Arabic-numbered fields, in such a manner that the number 1 could be found in the right-hand lower field, and the number 16 in the upper left field. The magic, or oddity, consisted in the fact that these numbers, regardless of how they were added up, from the top down, across, or diagonally, would always yield the sum of 34.[3] Such was the conformation, when translated into analogous temporal relationships, of the *strenge Satz*, the strict compositional style in which each element is given its full sway, yet can attain to its full meaning only as an integral part of the whole work.

Reflecting on the implications of his friend's approach to music, Zeitblom expresses his considered opinion that ". . . when the composer actually gets down to work, he is no longer free." Adrian, by way of countering such a stricture, offers his own contradictory definition of freedom: ". . . bound by a self-created compulsion for order, hence free" (p. 254). Zeitblom knows — and he is most uneasy with his knowledge — that such a paradox is the crucible of his friend's creative energies. Yet as a humanist he cannot come to grips with it, and is reduced to floundering in helpless clichés, such as ". . . well, yes, the dialectic of freedom is unfathomable" (p. 254). What Zeitblom does not know — or perhaps does not wish to know — is that his friend means to leave the last residue of societal intercourse behind him and to reach for a transcendent mode of being where absolute license and absolute compulsion have coalesced into synonymity. The freedom offered by absolute organization lies on the far side of the "breakthrough," in a realm not accessible except through daemonic assistance.

The lust for "breaking through" is contagious in *Doctor Faustus*. Notions of Germany breaking out into world preeminence have begun to be fostered in gatherings of elitist groups. Fervent advocacies of a national renewal to be nourished by a return to barbarism begin to take hold and to contribute to an eventual plunge into Hitlerism.[4] Central to the novel's action, however, is the breakthrough as it applies to musical composition and indeed to the novel itself, whose fabric is stretched to its limits and beyond, as it toys with the structural absolute envisioned by the protagonist.

Early in the novel, there is an allusion to the penchant for breaking out of one's proper and prescribed sphere: Zeitblom recollects how Johann Leverkühn, Adrian's father, had provided entertainment for his

---

[3] *D.F.*, p. 125.

[4] For an illuminating exposition of the theme of revolution through reaction, see Joseph Frank, "Reaction as Progress: Thomas Mann's *Dr. Faustus*," in *The Widening Gyre* (New Brunswick, N.J.), pp. 131-161.

young son and other children by amazing them with "voracious drops" of oil or chloroform suspended in water, or by causing a thin layer of sand spread over a vibrating glass plate to arrange itself in patterns of "visible music." Here Adrian's friend plays with the common root in German of "attempting" and "tempting":

> But to manipulate nature, to elicit phenomena from her, to "tempt" her by laying bare her workings by means of experiments; all this had something to do with witchcraft, indeed belonged in that realm and was itself the work of the "tempter," such was the persuasion of earlier epochs: a respectable point of view, if you ask me.[5]

By an ingenious play on etymologies Mann is able to evoke the ambiguous and suspect activities of an alchemist, though Leverkühn senior himself is a most upstanding burgher and exemplary father afflicted with nothing more than a mild headache. The conjured-up alchemist can only be Faustus, the restless 16th-century magician who experimented with the possibility of a "breakthrough" and ended in hellfire. Inevitably, the creation of music and literature entails a reorganization of time. The pace of a literary plot and the beat of music draw the reader and listener into a new rhythm and, once caught up in it, the eventual reentry into clock-time may be a jarring experience. Aside from such general characteristics common to these two arts, Adrian's conception of musical structure — and hence the organization of Mann's novel as well — embodies an overriding tendency toward "verticality" which is at odds with the horizontal axis along which the temporal arts must unfold. The tenacious struggle for the reconciliation of the unreconcilable is characteristic of *Doctor Faustus* and at the heart of its tragic mode.

Almost twenty-five years had elapsed since the publication of *The Magic Mountain*, the other large-scale narrative by Mann informed by an intense preoccupation with time.[6] A passage from a lecture in English delivered at Princeton University and later appended to the American edition of the novel, describes the author's remembered intention very well:

---

[5] "Daß nun gar das Unterfangen, mit der Natur zu laborieren, sie zu Phänomenen zu reizen, sie zu "versuchen," indem man ihr Wirken durch Experimente bloßstellt, — daß das alles ganz nahe mit Hexerei zu tun habe, ja schon in ihren Bereich falle und selbst ein Werk des "Versuchers" sei, war die Überzeugung früherer Epochen: eine respektable Überzeugung, wenn man mich fragt." *D.F.*, p. 28.

[6] For the best analysis of the time structure in this novel, see Hermann J. Weigand, *Thomas Mann's Novel 'Der Zauberberg'* (New York, 1933), pp. 14-24.

The book depicts the hermetic enchantment of its young hero within the timeless, and thus seeks to abrogate time itself by means of the technical device that attempts to give complete presentness at any given moment to the entire world of ideas that it comprises. It tries, in other words, to establish a magical *nunc stans*, to use a formula of the scholastics.[7]

Here Mann locates the roots of his endeavor in the scholasticism of the Christian Middle Ages, though much in the narrative technique proper — that aspect of it which creates the feeling of a continuing presentness — grew out of his early veneration of the music of Richard Wagner. It was that composer's *Leitmotiv* technique which served Mann as a model for repetitive patterns, arranged and modulated with the greatest narrative virtuosity.

Even in as early a novella as *Tonio Kröger* (1903), such reiterated phrases as "we are not gypsies in a green wagon," or the repetition, at moments of psychic stock-taking, of Tonio softly whistling to himself and of tilting his head to one side, serve to arrest the forward movement of the narrative and to bring about a conflation of emotionally similar moments in the past. The stages in the development of this technique, with which Mann has become so closely identified, show a remarkable growth in complexity and sophistication. The early verbal parallelisms are deepened and transformed into thematic and symbolic congruences. Thus in *The Magic Mountain* we see Pribislav Hippe's mechanical pencil become the vehicle which serves to connect a tentatively intimate encounter in Hans Castorp's childhood with the adult Walpurgis-night eroticism on the Magic Mountain. Through the crackling of the x-ray machinery in the sanatorium's lower reaches, the pervasive theme of death is brought home to the reader, and again when we share with Castorp a glimpse into the shadowy contours of Madame Chauchat's chest cavity, and yet again, marvel along with him at the intricate bone structure of his own hand as it emerges on the screen of the fluoroscope.

There is, however, in *The Magic Mountain*, at least one instance of arrested temporal progression which is evoked by means other than the repetition of motifs. This occurs in the chapter named "Snow", in which the historic span of an entire civilization and — by a kind of symbolic transfer — the substance of the novel are gathered up in a single, visionary moment.

The narration has reached a point where the "moist spot" in Castorp's lung has almost dried up, though after two years in the sanatorium the healing process is still not complete. He grows restless and feels a sudden impulse to break away from the daily hospital routine. Against the doctor's orders he prepares to embark on a wintry escapade; he straps

---

[7] *The Magic Mountain* (New York, 1958), p. 725.

on a pair of skis which he had earlier learned to maneuver tolerably well, and then pushes off toward unfamiliar ground. In winter, the weather in the mountains above Davos is notoriously uncertain, and Hans is not greatly surprised when the skies darken and he finds himself in the midst of a blinding snowstorm. Having acquired a certain amount of mountain lore, he doggedly adheres to a straight course up and down several slopes, only to discover, just as he confidently expects to be approaching the sanatorium, the hay shelter which he had passed when the storm first broke. He had moved in a large circle, "just as the books say" (he tells himself). Now at least he can find some protection under the hut's overhanging roof. The prolonged exposure to the bitter cold has exhausted him. As he leans against the shelter wall, seeking protection beneath the projecting roof from the swirling snow, he soon falls into a sleep-like trance. A pleasing vision begins to pervade his numbed senses, and brightly lit vistas of balmy Mediterranean shores appear before his entranced soul. He sees "children of the sun" engaged in a bustling life along the fertile slopes of a mountainous littoral, each happily performing his natural task; and just as the harmonious communal life appears in its most idyllic serenity, the dream image glides from the open countryside into the dark recesses of a pagan temple where mythical hags are engaged in dismembering a child's body, in consummation of a barbaric propitiary rite. A shaken Hans Castorp comes to know the price exacted by the furies. He awakens and begins to survey his situation. The snow has ceased to fall and the skies have cleared. As he returns to full consciousness, he is convinced that many days or weeks have passed since he lost his bearings in the storm. The vision which has been granted the dreamer seems as though it could only have come to one whose life has been a long journey toward wisdom; and one can understand that Castorp is startled when he looks at his pocket watch — the old, reliable time-piece inherited from his father — and finds that only a few minutes have passed since he has reached the hut, a mere moment into which the vast panoply of his dream vision is compressed. Here is how Mann renders Castorp's awakening:

> Amazing! Could it be that he had lain here in the snow only ten minutes or so and that he had spun out those scenes of horror and delight, and these reckless thoughts . . .?[8]

A dream, a temporary uncoupling of the controls governing wakeful behavior, has brought about the condition of the "magical nunc stans." It is surely a privileged moment that casts its spell backward and forward over the entire novel, a writer's master stroke which elicited a

---

[8] *Der Zauberberg*, 4th ed. (Berlin and Frankfurt, 1960), p. 454.

noteworthy observation by Hermann Weigand, in his influential work dealing exclusively with Mann's novel: "Hovering there between life and death, Hans Castorp is for a moment elevated to a position of clarity that marks the acme of his capacity to span the poles of cosmic experience."[9]

Indeed, *The Magic Mountain* represents a majestic effort at mastery over time. While there is a readily accessible linearity in the events occurring over a period of seven years, the novel also pushes toward an abrogation of its own successive nature. A *nunc stans* is certainly evoked, but its full force is reserved for one central episode which cannot — and probably should not — endow all the major occurrences of the story with the capacity to become part of an encompassing "vertical chord." The moment in the "Snow" chapter is the exclusive possession of Hans Castorp and lacks the capacity to dislodge the rest of the narrative from its carefully plotted temporal axis. To be sure, perceived duration before and after this chapter expands and contracts according to the manner in which events impinge on Castorp's consciousness. But no matter how brief a day or how fleeting a year on the Mountain may seem, it is always the psychological response to time which is at issue and not its metaphysical or mystical transcendence.

In the planning and execution of *Doctor Faustus* — a process concerning which the author affords the reader some insight in the little volume *The Story of a Novel: The Genesis of Doctor Faustus*[10] — considerably more was at stake than the creation of yet another version of the famous legend. It constituted in fact another — and surely a final — confrontation with the *nunc stans*, an attempt to arrive at a more radical solution to the problem with which he had grappled in *The Magic Mountain*. Mann communicates some of the fervor and even feelings of recklessness which accompanied the writing of *Doctor Faustus* in passages like this:

> A work of art is always conceived as a single whole, and even though according to aesthetic philosophy a work of verbal and musical art — as distinct from one in the visual arts — is necessarily temporal and sequential in nature, it yet strives to be completely *there* at every moment.[11]

The gulf between temporality and an enduring present tense could be emotionally and provisionally bridged by various tricks available to a writer, — certainly to an accomplished technician like Mann — but unless there could be a "breakthrough" arising from the very core of

[9] Hermann J. Weigand, *op. cit.*, p. 23.

[10] *Die Entstehung des Doktor Faustus* (Amsterdam, 1949).

[11] *Ibid.*, p. 154. Italics mine.

the work, nothing new of great importance would have been created. Leverkün's presumption was his Faustian *hubris*. The *Augenblick* could be attained only through a pact with the devil. The reckless grandeur of Leverkühn's ambition was matched by the dimension of the final catastrophe. But Adrian's own limits also point to the frontiers of literature along which his verbal artificer was moving.

Significantly, in view of his innate bent for transcendence, Leverkühn had begun by studying theology, and as could be expected from his habit of parodying the Mephistophelian bearing of one of his teachers — one Eberhard Schleppfuss — he came to be on intimate terms with Satan. He often enjoyed Zeitblom's discomfiture when he reeled off a catalogue of arcane and pithy names for the devil which he had absorbed from the vernacular of the more devil-conscious ambience of Martin Luther's century, from "Divel" to "Timothy Tempter" to "Father of Lies."[12] But the earliest and most decisive influence on Adrian's spirit had been his father, who foreshadowed with his demonstrations what his son would fulfill in the realm of musical composition. Through his music Adrian sought to convey himself into a forbidden state of eternal presentness, where the most extreme oppositions — including that between total organization and total freedom — are fused into a seamless unity. Whether the vision of such a goal takes on the form of an "all in One" as in Plotinus, or as an "all-encompassing center" as in *The Book of Twenty-Four Philosophers*, or as the "maximum in the minimum" as in Nicholas de Cusa, it is always an attempt to overcome the gap between human reality and a mystically illumined human potential.

From the standpoint of the outcome, Leverkühn is closely related to Johann Faustus, the German folk hero-sinner of the sixteenth century who, unlike Goethe's Faust, must go to hell after twenty-four years of earthly glory and power. But the parallel with the Renaissance Faustus is not the whole picture, because the radicalism of Mann's narrative experiment also brings to mind Goethe's more modern drama and its pivotal life-and-death wager for the fulfilled moment. The paradoxical union between freedom and compulsion inherent in Leverkühn's conception of musical composition, which had so baffled his friend, applies with equal force to Mann's composition in words. The "strict compositional style" (*strenger Satz*) of the novel itself bears witness to this fact. Clearly it was Mann's intention to have the musical metaphor suffuse the novel to the point of virtual identity, as can be seen in a diary entry:

[12] Designations used by H.T. Lowe-Porter, Mann's English translator, to approximate German names for the devil, such as "Teixel," "Meister Klepperlin," "der Widersacher," and several others.

Indeed I sensed that my book was itself bound to become that of which it treated, namely constructivist music.[13]

Mann deliberately invested the discussions on compositional method with sufficient specific detail to make them convincing as applications of authentic music theory, and yet he was careful not to become so involved in technicalities as to make the metaphoric transfer to literature difficult or impossible.[14]

One is tempted to say therefore that it was not only Leverkühn who was hell-bent on breaking out of the dead end of parody which he judges the history of music to have reached; but that it was also Thomas Mann who, nearing the age where each new enterprise was likely to be his last, wagered on achieving the impossible transcendence. Unlike a true mystic, however, the novelist did not burn his bridges. An overall ironic stance, above all the ironic distancing between himself and the narrator and *a forteriori* between himself and the protagonist, allowed him to keep one foot firmly planted in the pragmatic terrain of concrete temporality.

It is well to point to Mann's lifelong preoccupation with artist figures, such as Hanno Buddenrook and Tonio Kröger, and even Cipolla in *Mario and the Magician*. They are, each in their own way, "creators" marked by forbidden knowledge, divorced from the mainstream of communal life, and sometimes in truck with criminality. Leverkühn, the Faustian alchemist of music, represents the final link in the long chain of Mannian artists. His reckless experiment exacts its price in the currencies of life, so that he is cut off from the animal warmth of closeness and love, and from the comforts to be derived from a personal commitment to those nearest him.

The novel's vehicle for its foray into transcendence is the very thing to be transcended: consecutive musical notes and time-bound verbal assemblages. They are to be crystallized into a transparent structure that will absorb their temporal progression and become the *kairos* of an encompassing still point. The powers summoned to bring about this transmutation are those of artistic genius. With success in any ultimate sense forever out of reach, its unwavering pursuit in the face of hopelessness gives to the work its characteristic dimensions of irony and tragedy.

The "constructivist" design and strict compositional style of *Doctor Faustus* require that its center be everywhere. Adrian puts it this way:

---

[13] *Die Entstehung des Doktor Faustus*, p. 49.

[14] The relationship between compositional theory and Mann's structural technique in the novel has been convincingly demonstrated by Gunilla Bergsten in her book *Thomas Mann's Doctor Faustus* (Chicago, 1969), pp. 164, 168. Mann's controversy with Arnold Schönberg lies outside the scope of this study.

[The basic motif] is like a word, a key word, whose presence can be felt everywhere in the song which it wishes to determine entirely . . . every note in the composition as a whole would have to justify itself, both melodically and harmonically, regarding its connection to the predetermined basic series.[15]

Indeed, the motif is sounded in the first few pages of the novel, with the image of a rare butterfly which inhabits the rain forests of the Amazon basin. When Adrian was still a child, he was shown a picture of it, rendered in resplendent colors, on a page of a luxurious volume filled with all manner of small exotic creatures. The insect's scientific name, *Hetaera Esmeralda*, duly listed beneath its likeness, sounded as alluringly strange as its appearance was dazzling to the young boy. Several butterflies belonging to this species — so the father had lectured to his rapt audience — protected themselves against their natural enemies not by mimicry, but by a ready supply of foul-smelling and poisonous secretions. Their predators had learned to avoid such baited prey, and hence Esmeralda and her kind had no need for camouflage. On the contrary, their best defense — sufficient for their survival as a species — was to flutter about as conspicuously as possible. Zeitblom is moved to offer his own schoolmasterly commentary as he records the idyllic scene showing father Leverkühn leafing through the illustrations and dazzling the children with his knowledge of the many wonders of nature: "The manifold conjunctions among things! — Poison and beauty, poison and magic. . . . Even if [we children] could not reason it out then, still Jonathan Leverkühn conveyed the general sense of it" (*D.F.*, p. 26). The butterfly's name and function, transmuted, reversed, alluded to, or symbolized, arises from deep within the fabric of the narrative and becomes inextricably interwoven with the threads that lie closer to the surface. Most important, Esmeralda will become the name which Adrian, as a young man, will bestow upon a prostitute whom he visits in a bordello and to whose body he is irresistibly drawn. The strength of his ardor is such that it brings about a heightening of the prostitute's soul to an almost angelic compassion for her client-lover. She warns him of the danger hidden in her blood and tries in vain to dissuade her visitor from embracing her. But Adrian's path is marked. He must embark on a "God-tempting venture," and move into a terrain where the punishment is comprised in the sin. Swarms of syphilis spirochetes will later

---

[15] "[Das Grundmotiv] ist wie ein Wort, ein Schlüsselwort, dessen Zeichen überall in dem Lied zu finden sind und es gänzlich determinieren möchten. . . . Jeder Ton der gesamten Komposition, melodisch und harmonisch, müßte sich über seine Beziehung zu dieser vorbestimmten Grundreihe auszuweisen haben." *D.F.* p. 255.

whip his powers to a fever pitch, until their "breakthrough" into cerebral tissues marks his commitment to the fires of hell.

When Adrian was twenty-seven, midway through his life and halfway through the novel, he spent a summer in the ancient Italian hill-town of Palestrina, located in the Sabine hills south of Rome. It is here that he had his encounter with Satan himself. Zeitblom informs the reader that he found an account of the terrible confrontation among his friend's papers. It was written by Leverkühn in the German Baroque idiom to which he liked to turn in moments of crisis. The document therefore reaches the reader from a level at several removes from the surface of the story itself. It calls to mind the devil's crassly wicked machinations described in late sixteenth-century chapbooks, and is reminiscent also — mainly in its idiosyncratic diction — of Eberhard Schleppfuss, lecturer in theology, whose mimicking of the earthy Lutheran manner of speech had delighted Adrian during his student years. When the visitation with the devil took place, four years had elapsed since he had embraced Esmeralda, an occurrence, as the infernal guest insisted, that had sealed his pact with him. Since such a contractual arrangement with Satan must run the traditional course of twenty-four years, Adrian was left with twenty years of life when he returned to Munich from his sojourn in Italy. Those who have read the novel to the end know that in fact only ten years of creative life are left to him before his mind succumbs to the spirochete invasion.

The taxonomic designation *hetaera esmeralda* is a felicitous discovery Mann's.[16] Beyond its basic significations of butterfly and concubine, beauty and poison, the name provides the matrix for a "constructivist" tonal row consisting of the notes h, e, a, e, es (English: b, e, a, e, e-flat), the sequence which appears in numerous permutations in Adrian's compositions and which functions as the structural axis around which the novel's interlocking rings revolve. It is the basic motif in terms of which all aspects of the novel must justify themselves, and the key word for the "strict compositional style," practiced by both the protagonist and his author. *Hetaera*, moreover, the source of migraine, and of majestic mental powers, hearth of disease and the scourge of genius, provides the schema for the *nunc stans* which is to absorb all temporal manifestations of the novel. Both substance and structure are indebted to Esmeralda. Adrian's migraine is a symptom of the advancing syphilis infection, as well as an analogue to the more benign headache of which

---

6 For a discussion of Mann's source, see Calvin S. Brown, "The Entomological Source of Mann's Poisonous Butterfly," *Germanic Review*, XXXVII (January, 1962), 116-120.

his father, the owner of the picture book of exotic butterflies, had complained. Similarly, Adrian's various places of residence are made to coalesce into a simultaneous, multi-leveled presence. The village of Buchel, the composer's childhood home, has its counterpart in the homestead near the Bavarian town of Pfeiffering, the retreat of his mature years. There is no reason to think that the two localities would seem at all similar to the eyes of a neutral observer, but they become remarkably congruent when they appear as superimposed images in the mind's eye of the hero, of a fervently sympathetic narrator, and hence of the reader. The environment of his childhood, the farm building with its venerable tree in front, the pond to one side of it, and the chained watchdog barking furiously at approaching strangers, all share in the emergence of a basic pattern within which specific temporal events become manifest. Adrian is keenly aware of the power of such congruences and of their efficacy in imprinting themselves on his psyche. For example, he is prompted to address the watchdog — with whom he soon establishes a particularly friendly rapport — as "Suso," the name of the canine sentry of his childhood, though he knows fullwell that the dog's present name, given him by the owners of the Pfeiffering farmstead, is "Kaschperl." In the course of a few weeks, all the dwellers on the farm learn to say "Suso," and when the animal no longer responds to the call of "Kaschperl," the conflation of past and present is complete.

The analogy — even to the point of metaphorical identity — between musical composition and Mann's narrative procedure is made explicit in the text and in the author's explanatory remarks about his novel *Doctor Faustus*, however, is after all not music but literature, and unmetaphorically shares its structure and temporal progression with other literary fictions. For this reason, it should not surprise us if the insights of Auerbach's "Figura" essay have explanatory value for Mann's novel as well, even though the essay deals not with a modern novel, but with Christian exegesis of Scripture and with an exemplary medieval work of religious poetry. The major stages and characters in Mann's novel meet all the requirements — translated into their secular equivalents — of Auerbach's essay; each event or character is palpably present and occupies the appropriate place in the "providential" scheme of the novel's development, and attains to its full and many-layered meaning only when it is interpreted as a fulfillment of the past and a foreshadowing of a future "higher" realization. The important markers in the plotted progression of the novel are representative of the entire story. Each is a pinpoint and ubiquitous center, containing the work *in nuce* in a fusion of content and meaning. *Hetaera esmeralda*, the watchdog Suso, the twelve-tone row of Adrian's breakthrough — these are structurally not far removed from Beatrice, Satan's three faces, and the *terza rima*, no matter how vastly Dante's meanings differ from Mann's. Dante's famous lines which open the second canto of the Inferno serve as an epigraph to the novel, and we know from Mann's published comments that when he labored toward the conclusion of his book, he reread Dante with special intensity in preparation for the culminating chapters.[17] Indeed in the novel itself, Serenus Zeitblom refers repeatedly to the *Divine Comedy* and to Adrian's special kinship with its visionary symmetries.[18]

It will be useful to single out the main strands threading their way through the narrative, so that we may know what it is that becomes part of the stupendously complex "chord" which would summon up the work's meaning at the instant of its sounding. Adrian's life spans the years 1885 to 1940. Zeitblom begins to write his biography in May 1943 and completes it in 1945. The two years devoted to the recording of the composer's life are also the last years of Nazi rule over Germany, so that the pages dealing with Adrian's final descent into madness are written to the accompaniment of a cataclysmic rain of Allied bombs, and during the death throes of Zeitblom's beloved fatherland. From the beginning, the reader can easily follow three stories which intermittently rise to the surface and are placed in polyphonic rapport with one another: Adrian's life story; his friend's service to that life, which includes the labor of setting it down for posterity; and third, the historical events leading to Germany's defeat in World War II, including the stages of that apocalyptic process.

All the other temporal sequences — whether they pertain to individuals or groups — achieve to their full function only in relation to the three dominant stories. It is not difficult to discern the historical and intellectual developments which run parallel to Leverkühn's life. The earlier phases of German history — the Middle Ages and the Renaissance — are conveyed mainly by architectural styles characteristic of old German cities and by the intellectual atmosphere associated with Adrian's sojourns in places like Kaisersaschern, Halle, Leipzig, Munich and Pfeiffering. Nor is the history of the German language excluded from the "chord." The Lutheran and Faustian idiom are brought to life through the antiquarian speech mannerisms of Adrian's theology professor and later through Adrian's zestful parody of them. The highly encapsulated, carefully modulated and syntactically bracing sentences of Serenus Zeitblom recall the German academic style of the late nineteenth century, while a fashionable "re-barbarized" conversational idiom prevails among the intellectuals and pseudo-intellectuals who gather in the sumptuous homes of Munich's leading citizens.

---

[17] See *Die Entstehung des Doktor Faustus*, p. 111.

[18] See for example chp. xx, p. 215; chp. xxxiv, p. 476 (pp. 163 and 358 in the U.S. edition).

One can describe the pervasive "all-at-once" tendency in the novel without touching on the venerable association between the "fulfilled moment" on the one hand and infinite circles or spheres on the other. For the "Twenty-Four Philosophers" and for Nicholas de Cusa, as we have seen, the all-encompassing point was an infinitely compressed sphere, containing the maximum in the minimum. In Mann's novel not very much is made of the symbolic force of circularity. Still, there is one passage which, while seemingly somewhat apart from the main-stream of the narrative, sounds that motif in a quaint and original fashion, thus linking the novel — more explicitly than elsewhere — to a tenacious hermetic tradition.

In the twenty-seventh chapter, more than halfway through the novel we learn that Adrian, whose reputation was by that time well-established among a small circle of avant-garde connoisseurs, has provided a musical setting for the poem "Spring Festival" ("*Frühlingsfeier*") by Friedrich Klopstock (1724-1803). It is a long paean to spring which had enjoyed great popularity in the eighteenth century.[19] In the first two strophes of the unrhymed, Miltonizing verses, the earth is referred to as a mere "drop in the bucket," compared to the vastness of the universe:

> Nicht in den Ozean der Welten alle
> Will ich mich stürzen! schweben nicht,
> Wo die ersten Erschaffnen, die Jubelchöre der Söhne des Lichts,
> Anbeten, tief anbeten und in Entzückung vergehn!

> Nur um den Tropfen am Eimer,
> Um die Erde nur will ich schweben und anbeten!
> Halleluja! Halleluja! Der Tropfen am Eimer
> Rann aus der Hand des Allmächtigen auch!

> Not into the ocean of all the worlds
> Will I plunge! I will not soar
> Where the first-created, the jubilant choirs of the sons of light,
> Worship, worship in deep-stirring passion, and melt in their bliss!

> Merely about the drop in the bucket,
> Merely about the earth will I soar, worshipping!
> Hallelujah! Hallelujah! For even the drop in the bucket
> Fell from the hand of the Almighty!

With this, Klopstock, imbued with the enthusiasm of eighteenth-century pietism, found himself on familiar biblical ground, for he had the verses of Isaiah 40:15 in mind:

---

[19] The poem is referred to in an early episode of Goethe's *Werther*. A spring landscape after a cleansing thunder shower instantly evokes Klopstock's poem in the minds of both Werther and Lotte.

Behold, the nations are as a drop of a bucket,
and are counted as the small dust of the balance:
behold, he taketh up the isles as a very little thing.

In the geocentric, biblical perspective, it is nations and islands which
are like drops of water or grains of dust. In Klopstock's poem, the metaphorical leap in the *Isaiah* verses has been extended to the whole earth
as a celestial body. Having been displaced, some two centuries before
the poem was written, from its central cosmic stage, our planet could
well be seen as the inadvertently spilled "drop in a bucket." While the
metaphoric scope of the drop is expanded to astronomic dimensions, its
physical minuteness is thereby made more strikingly evident, and the
poet's faith in its stature as an object of jubilant adoration all the more
touching.

However, Adrian's musical setting of "Spring Festival" is no ordinary
tribute to Klopstock. It is in fact a tribute in reverse, in the sense that
the music amounts to a "taking back" of the poet's exuberant humility.
Where Klopstock would be too humble to "plunge" or "soar too far
from the earth," there Leverkühn's musical structures brashly presume
to exist in the midst of the "ocean of all the worlds." Zeitblom is uncomfortably aware of the inverse relationship between the text of the poem
and its musical setting. To his humanistic concerns and values the void
of cosmic space offers nothing but cold and impenetrable indifference.
His comment as narrator makes clear his downright antipathy to the
monstrous scale and inhuman dimensions of the universe:

> The data of cosmic creation are nothing but a deafening bombardment of our
> intelligence by numbers equipped with a comet's tail of some two dozen zeros
> which comport themselves as if they somehow had something to do with
> human reason and measure.[20]

Zeitblom feels at ease with Klopstock's more circumscribed vision.
Within the poem's pious context, he deems the comparison between the
earth and "the drop" to be particularly apt not only because of their
similar shape, but also because, as is well known, three quarters of the
globe's surface consists of water. This somewhat hackneyed and comfortably correct observation prompts Adrian to spin out a fanciful tale
of deep-sea exploration. The two friends find themselves in the austere
environment of the "abbot's room" at Pfeiffering when Adrian regales
his weekend guest with reminiscences of his friendship with one Professor Capercailzie, the famous deep-sea explorer. Together with him —
so Adrian asserts while puffing on his cigar — he had entered the hollow

---

[20] *D.F.*, p. 361.

interior of the cunningly engineered bathysphere and descended 250C
feet toward the bottom of the sea. At that depth he was able to observe
at close range numerous monstrously shaped creatures, some of them
glowing with an eerie self-generated luminosity, as they passed by the
observation window. The diving bell, constructed to withstand
immense pressure, was in fact a hollow sphere,[21] a structural necessity
which provides the teller of this adventure story with an opportunity to
comment on the "drop in the bucket" — only this time not by way of
a musical setting, but from the vantage point of homespun psychology
Making use of the awe before the infinite space of the cosmos, so mov
ingly evident in Klopstock's poem, Adrian abruptly abandons his fic
titious descent into deep waters in favor of an intellectual foray into
galactic regions. With feigned ingenuousness he speaks of "our" pla
netary system and "our" galaxy, thus adding an ironic double bottom
to any facile intimacy with astral phenomena. Adrian knows, and has
painfully experienced, the human need for living within protective
enclosures which, when extended to the stars, usually manifest them
selves in the form of circles and spheres. He goes on to express his
conviction that, in this psychological sense, all men have passed their
days in the protective geometry of a hollow sphere (p. 359).[22] If the
"drop in the bucket" could be adored, as in Klopstock's poem (because
it too "fell from the hand of the Almighty"), then its structural function
is much like that of a key word in the context of a "strict" musical o
verbal composition. The infinitesimal drop and the bucketful of water
are in polar opposition to each other, much like the ubiquitous cente
and the infinite sphere. Klopstock's "Spring Festival," with its quaintly
forlorn drop of water, thus offers itself as a tenuous link between
Mann's *Dr. Faustus* and the tradition of mystical geometry exemplified
by Plotinus, Nicholas Cusanus, Giordano Bruno and Pascal. The novel'
concern throughout most of the narrative is not with circularity but with
the compression of linear successiveness into simultaneity. As we have
seen, one important Western tradition envisions such a transcenden
nunc stans as a non-dimensional point, holding within itself all that i
contained in the infinite sphere of which it is the center. Only once in
the novel did Mann see fit to draw from this tradition of circularity and
to make it into a somewhat "off-beat" fictional reality.

The spiritual stages traversed by Leverkühn are artfully made to cor
respond with those subsumed under the larger spans of German intel
lectual history beginning with the Renaissance, while the evolution o

---

[21] "Eine kugelförmige Taucherkugel" (p. 355). In the Lowe-Porter translation th
adjective is mistakenly translated as "bullet-shaped," ignoring the important sym
bolic function of the vessel's spherical shape.
[22] "In dieser Geborgenheit, einer tief inneren Geborgenheit, scheint die Neigun
der Natur zum Sphärischen sich durchzusetzen" (p. 359).

music in the Christian era, rendered in depth and detail, reaches back to its more distant origins in medieval church liturgy. Secular, instrumental music is shown as it relates to several national traditions; but here too, beginning with the eighteenth century, Mann's focus narrows to the German scene, which is seen as culminating in the encompassing mastery of Beethoven. Like German political history, and like the novel itself, the history of music is ruled by the force of its apocalypse. The higher the level of its evolution, the sooner it will reach the point when it can no longer yield genuinely new configurations; only variations, or "parodies" of what once was new, are possible. For Adrian, music had in fact reached this final stage. To overcome and transcend the bounds of its historicity and to burst into the realm of the absolute, that was the goal in the light of which the prospect of hellfire paled to insignificance. The "taking back" of Klopstock's "Spring Festival" was a mere rehearsal compared to Leverkühn's last opus, *Fausti Wehklage (The Lamentation of Dr. Faustus)*. This work is described as being strongly reminiscent of Beethoven's Ninth Symphony, above all by virtue of its interweaving of orchestral and choral passages, so that Zeitblom begins to recognize that his friend's final composition ". . . moves, so to speak, in a direction opposite to the 'Ode to Joy'; it is the *negativum*, of co-equal genius, of the transition of the symphony into vocal jubilation. It is the taking back. . . .,"[23] an abrogation of Beethoven amounting to a profound schism in the development of music, perhaps even to a denial of the possibility of original musical composition, and by extension, of the possibility of literary creation as well.

Adrian himself becomes a symbol — a chord-like instantaneous presence — of German music, and also the focal point of the sickness of a nation possessed by the devil. But as a twentieth-century Faustus, Adrian is also representative of Western man bent on "speculating the elements," inclined to a "re-barbarization" of the arts and rocketing toward an instantaneous ubiquity.

---

[23] *D.F.*, p. 649.

Chapter Seven

OVERVIEW

What is certain and incredible, is that all the enormous
palace was, in its most minute details, there in the poem,
with each illustrious porcelain and each design on each
porcelain and the penumbrae and the light of each dawn
and twilight, and each unfortunate or happy instant in the
glorious dynasties of mortals, of gods and dragons that had
inhabited it from the unfathomable past.

JORGE LUIS BORGES, "PARABLE OF THE PALACE"

To mention Hermes Trismegistus and Plotinus along with Thomas
Mann and Samuel Beckett, in one breath as it were, makes light of the
progressions and regressions of history. But because the all-encompassing pinpoint, or center, has been an effectively available notion over an
enormous span of European intellectual history, such simplification may
clear the way to seeing the matter in high relief. The permutations of
the circle and center have been recorded and admirably described by
Dietrich Mahnke in his book on the "infinite sphere and all-encompassing circle" (*Unendliche Sphäre und Allmittelpunkt*).[1] Unfortunately
Mahnke's study was not given a great deal of scholarly attention; it
deserved better. Now, almost a century after its publication — and even
after Georges Poulet's important *Metamorphoses of the Circle* — we still
await a new historical account dealing with the ancient image.

In our study, the historical vicissitudes of the image appear but sket-
chily, if at all, in the background. All attention is directed to the recur-
ring pattern itself as it becomes manifest in Western thought and poetry.

---

[1] See note 12, p. 32 above.

Today — no less than in the Middle Ages — it is testimony to an undiminished impatience with the inexorable, tick-tock successiveness of chronicity. The symptoms of this particular discomfiture have not yet been taken fully into account with respect to literature, and a cogent interpretation of them has been my goal.

In his *Poetics*, Aristotle had taught that tragedy, as well as the other kinds of poetic writing then practiced, represented a discrete sequence of occurrences — a "praxis" or "action" of a certain size — of which the beginning and ending could be determined by the application of logic. That view remained essentially intact through many centuries of European literary history. By and large, the great poets were moral and religious teachers who instructed and pleased most effectively by *mimesis*, that is, by "holding up the mirror to nature." It was not until well into the eighteenth century that the artist began to be seen in a different light and that his function changed accordingly. He became the vessel of a higher inspiration, a prophet-like figure and a "genius" who as an artist stood in close communion with divine powers not accessible to ordinary men.

Not surprisingly, a new understanding of poetic "making" began to inform literary theory and practice. The "mirror" of imitation gave way to "the lamp" of creative radiance.[2] Subjective images, rather than Aristotelian logic, revealed a discrete and unified nexus of events rounded out and delimited in so natural and organic a fashion that the question of beginnings and endings would scarcely arise. They had in common a special kind of coherence, an implicit vision of fulfilled moments, or according to Sartre's Roquentin in *La nausée*, an "adventure". Though human powers can never be quite equal to the task of fusing matter with meaning, or the concrete with the universal, the effort continues unabated to this day.

The birth and early life of "the pinpoint of eternity" seems to coincide with the development of Christian dogma, as has been pointed out. In the *Divine Comedy* it appears as the central and most encompassing symbol: the pilgrim-poet Dante, having ascended to the highest and ultimate region of his purifying voyage, comes into the presence of the Lord, the all-encompassing, dimensionless node of light which, as it becomes clear to the studious reader through small shocks of belated recognition, had been a figured presence even in the lowest regions of the Inferno. As Dante is guided, so the reader is guided by the poet, from an indirect to a direct perception of "the center."

---

[2] See M.H. Abrams, *The Mirror and the Lamp: Romantic Theory and the Critical Tradition* (New York, 1953).

For Cusanus, the rational limits of his geometry were also the threshold of the infinite. Through heroic exertions, above all in the mathematical sciences, he attained to a level of "learned ignorance" which alone made possible a symbolic participation in the divine, just as the center of a circle is in radial rapport with its periphery. Man's soul was the preeminent "center," even though in the context of the traditional image, the center was "everywhere." The energy and exuberance of Cusanus' Renaissance humanism stood in stark contrast to the asceticism of the Middle Ages when flagellation of the flesh was seen as an appropriate preparation for life eternal.

Blaise Pascal also made the geometric image of the infinite circle his own. But between the center and the periphery he could see only the "*effroyable*" chasm of empty space. There were no spokes in the wheel of infinity. Without wagering on Christian faith to provide salvation, the most penetrating intellect would flounder hopelessly in nothingness.

In the age of enlightenment, the disciplines of mathematics and geometry became more and more self-contained, and their professors lost interest in the mystical and religious symbolism to which their quantitative operations had for so long lent support. But as a poetic *topos* the image of the infinite circle persisted and continues to flourish to this day. Either the circumference or the center, or simply "the point," are invoked as metaphors for infinite, and occasionally they appear united in a single figure.

The fulfilled *Augenblick*, the all-encompassing pinpoint of time, became the supreme value for Goethe's Faust figure. However, the attempt to compress time into an all-at-once presentness involved the deadly sin of *superbia*, of a *hubris* which arrogates the divine life to one's mortal self. Paradoxically, Faust's alliance with evil qualifies him in the end for the gift of grace. Hence in his egotistic dynamism, Faust became an exemplary quester, a paradigm of modern man's ruthless assault on the Absolute.

For Virginia Woolf as a novelist, the dreary successiveness of daily routine, the task of tracing a character's waking hours from breakfast through lunch to dinner, the alignment of activities with the weeks and months of the calendar, all these seemed to her a distraction from more essential matters. Yet she obviously thought it necessary to supply narrative markers which would move the plot forward and toward a conclusion. Her protagonists, however, do not attain to their true selves until they have freed themselves from the "leaden circles" of sound coming from London's Big Ben.

In a writer endowed with a narrative style responsive to minute movements and tremors of the psyche, it is startling to find that beneath the delicately wrought phrases there lurks a distrust, even a disenchantment, with words, so that Bernard — a fashioner of phrases much like the author — is seen, after all is said and done, to be longing for mono-syllables, for "a little language such as lovers use," a language, one sus-pects, of pre-lapsarian innocence, or of transcendence through death in the manner of Septimus Smith in *Mrs. Dalloway.* Yet Virginia Woolf was by no means as radical as a Samuel Beckett. She did not try to punctuate silence with fewer and fewer words, possibly because she experienced fulfillment and exhilaration from the full unfolding of her marvelous verbal gift, no matter if doubts about the reach and ultimate validity of language occasionally made themselves felt.

The plot of Thomas Mann's *Doctor Faustus* shows significant parallels to the chapbook, a Protestant zealot's lurid account of a necromancer's misdeeds which toward the end of the sixteenth century — and in a popular English translation — had proved so congenial to Christopher Marlowe's dramatic intentions. In the Elizabethan play, as in the chap-book, the hero enters into a pact with Mephistophilis which remained in force over a period of twenty-four years. Among the important dif-ferences between the older *Faust* story and Goethe's late eighteenth-century drama is that in the latter there is no pact. It was replaced by a wager without any time limitations. While Mann's *Doctor Faustus* adheres by and large to the older version — the twenty-four-year con-tract is maintained — one need not look far for evidence of the more modern Goethean tone. The "break-through" which Mann's hero, Adrian Leverkühn, seeks to achieve in the realm of musical composition is also a reckless quest for absolute freedom, above all freedom from bondage to tradition and "parody." Most important, it was Mann who, near the end of a renowned and arduous career, heroically reached out once more for the *Augenblick*, not as a single moment of epiphany, but as a constant concrete presentness through the pages of his last major novel. Accordingly, *hetaera esmeralda*, the poisonous butterfly endowed with extraordinary beauty, enjoys an actual, symbolic, or enciphered presence in all the important episodes of his *Doctor Faustus.*

We know that it is impossible to speak of a span of time without ultimately referring to a change in spatial relationships. Time and space imply one another. But it was the mystery of time rather than the equally mysterious dimensions of space that most fired the imagination during the Christian era. Our inability to surmount successiveness stands between us and the fulfilled moment. Such designations as "pin-point of eternity," the "maximum in the minimum," and the "eternal moment," are radical paradoxes whose resolutions are ardently desired and known to be forever beyond our grasp.

Among the indispensable evocations of this existential impasse in lit-erature is the "concrete universal." It has been my intention to show that the Hegelian "sensuous radiance of the idea" belongs in fact to the group of Paradoxical expressions consisting of the "pinpoint of eternity" and its synonyms. Like them, the Concrete Universal signals a craving for resolution, and implies the impossibility of satisfying it. Only an acceptance of some cardinal articles of Christian dogma, such as the Incarnation and Holy Communion, where matter and meaning are fused in perfect unity, can resolve the paradox. The logos does not *mean*; it *is*. In the Plotinian "intelligible" sphere, the world of discrete objects was distributed along the circumference, and all spirituality resided with the One at the center. Toward the beginning of the Renaissance, the sphere ceased being merely abstract or Platonically "intelligible"; it became "infinite" as well, and as a result, unlike its predecessor, could be accepted as an adequate representation of the physical universe, without detriment to its divine nature. It was through this image that the fusion of matter and spirit became possible. There was no longer any distinction between spiritual and physical centrality, as there still had been in Dante's cosmology. Now, in the realm of the newly "infinite" sphere, the succession of beginnings and endings were aspects of simultaneity, or modalities of an everlasting present tense. Not only is it impossible, in the circumscribed human condition, to bring about such a fusion, but the very attempt carries with it historical resonances of guilt, because such unholy experiments usurp a divine prerogative. This is the precise locus of Faust's transgression in Goethe's drama.

Without faith in an omnipotent governance and without a mystical certitude of a ubiquitous divine presence, we are condemned to a life of Sisyphus; the boulder will forever roll down again, and it is the hopeless exertion against overwhelming odds which is both absurd and necessary. "The struggle itself toward the heights," wrote Camus in his interpretation of the ancient myth, "is enough to fill a man's heart. One must imagine Sisyphus happy."[3] What is "struggle" to Camus is close to what Goethe liked to call "*handeln*," to be active, to work, referring specifically to the work of the poet which is required in order to fuse, if only for a moment of poetic ignition, the concrete with the universal. The lines in the second section of T.S. Eliot's "Burnt Norton" refer to this paradoxical situation:

> To be conscious is not to be in time
> But only in time can the moment in the rose-garden,
> The moment in the arbour where the rain beat,
> The moment in the draughty church at smokefall
> Be remembered; involved with past and future.
> Only through time time is conquered.

These verses are a necessary preparation for the fourth stanza which ends Eliot's quasi-Dantean vision of the center of eternity:

---

[3] *The Myth of Sisyphus and Other Stories*, trans. Justin O'Brien (New York, 1955), p. 91.

. . . After the kingfisher's wing
Has answered light to light, and is silent, the light is still
At the still point of the turning world.

Not every work of literature contains references to the problematic nature of time. Far from it. One would be hard put to find any particular concern with successiveness and simultaneity in Flaubert's *Madame Bovary* or in Dostoevski's *Crime and Punishment*. As writers they necessarily had to take account of the progression of time and organize their fictions in basic conformity with it; and yet, insofar as their works embody non-temporal meanings which hover over the successiveness of plotted events, they share in some sense with all other imaginative writings the imprint of the "still point."

Before we conclude our odyssey through post-Christian Western literature, we should not fail to observe various versions of the "pinpoint" in shorter, even minor works of the modern period and thereby obtain a sense of the continuing vitality of the motif.

A short story whose title leaves no doubt about its theme is E.M. Forster's *The Eternal Moment* (1905). It is a tale written in a gently ironic mode, dealing with the ingrained presumptions of English upper class society of the Victorian period and with the stubborn inability of its representatives to relate themselves to those whom they regard their social inferiors, except in ritualistic, master-servant behavior patterns. The "eternal moment" is not only the title of the story, but also that of a novel written by the story's protagonist, Miss Raby. As a young, well-to-do woman traveling on the Continent, she had stopped off at an idyllic Dolomite village called Vorta, located along the northern frontier of Italy bordering on Austria. There she had joined a party of adventurous English vacationers for a climb to the top of a nearby mountain. A local youth, named Feo Ginori, was hired to serve as a porter and guide, and it was this well-shaped mountain boy who, in a preposterous scene, had unknowingly provided Miss Raby's life with a luminous center. When she and Feo found themselves temporarily cut off and hidden from the other climbers, he had furtively seized her in a passionate embrace, stammering words of undying love. She had properly repulsed the youth's erotic foray and "thanked him not to insult her again."

In later years Miss Raby became a skillful writer of fiction. Her talent grew in scope and marketability as it drew nourishment from the recollected moment of near perfection. Her novel, "The Eternal Moment," was a poetic transformation of the incident which, though now hidden in a quasi-mystical glow, still had the vitality of actual experience.

The book became a huge popular success. Its subject matter promised to slake a Victorian thirst for forbidden pleasures, and the village of Vorta where Miss Raby had incautiously laid her story, soon became a favorite destination for English tourists. Fashionable hotels sprung up and vulgarized the once idyllic region.

After twenty years, the now famous authoress decided to indulge her quixotic wish to return to Vorta. She had to acknowledge to herself that

> . . . the incident upon the mountain had been one of the great moments of her life . . . perhaps the greatest, certainly the most enduring. . . . There was more reality in it than in all the years of success and varied achievement which had followed, and which had rendered it possible. A presumptuous boy had taken her to the gates of heaven; and though she would not enter with him, the eternal remembrance of the vision had made life seem endurable and good.[4]

She searched for and found Feo Ginori who, as she discovered to her somewhat pained amusement, had become an overweight *concierge* in one of the new hotels. Obedient to an irrepressible impulse, she confessed to him what his transgression of long ago had come to mean to her. Yet Miss Raby had lived to abandon the illusions of her youth and become accustomed to observing with a cold, objective eye even those things which affected her most intimately. Now Feo appeared to her as what he truly had become: an obsequious bore. Once this pathetic character had recovered from the shock of recognition, he only desired to turn the encounter to his and his burdensome family's financial advantage, a desire that Miss Raby knew how to satisfy — in a somewhat abstract gesture of contempt. She had come to know that "the moment" belonged to her alone. The mundane clumsiness which obscured the vision of sublimity only served to strengthen her sense of its preciousness.

In our age — under the continuing impact of romantic irony —poetic transcendencies of conventional temporal modes of perception are typically clothed in ironic modalities. The arcane evocations of George Luis Borges provide provocative variants. In a very brief prose piece, "Parable of the Palace," the "pinpoint" reaches us from an oriental never-never land, where the Yellow Emperor accompanies the poet through his palace and then journeys with him over the labyrinthine paths of his domain, leading over terraces which seem like "steps of an almost measureless amphitheater" which is traversed by many rivers, or perhaps many times by the same winding river. "At the foot of the penultimate tower" of the wall enclosing the emperor's lands, the poet composes his

4 *The Collected Tales of E.M. Forster* (New York, 1947), p. 300.

immortal poem of which the text has long been lost. Near the end of the Parable we read:

> There are some who contend [the poem] consisted of a single line; others say it had but a single word. The truth, the incredible truth, is that in the poem stood the enormous palace, entire and minutely detailed, with each illustrious porcelain and every sketch on every porcelain and the shadows and the lights of the twilights and each unhappy or joyous moment of the glorious dynasties of mortals, gods and dragons who had dwelled in it from the interminable past. All fell silent, but the emperor exclaimed, "You have robbed me of my palace!" And the executioner's iron sword cut the poet down.[5]

The tale had begun by advancing through traditional successive stages — only to end in an implosion of vast geographic regions and aeons of dynastic ages into a single word. Such a theft demanded imperial retribution.

The "pinpoint" appears again in the deceptively commonplace urban environment of the short story by Borges called *The Aleph*. Written in a comfortably realistic style, this first person narrative takes place in modern Buenos Aires. Public undertakings like urban renewal, as well as the vicissitudes of individual characters, are related as though from a stance of gently fatigued and reluctant involvement, until suddenly the "I" of the story, an indolent *littérateur*, finds himself face to face with the "ineffable center." This occurs while he is standing uncomfortably, and somewhat against his better judgment, on the steps of a stairway which leads from a trap door of his friend's kitchen down to a dank and cluttered cellar. He has gotten himself into that subterranean predicament because his friend had told him to look for the amazing Aleph. There, among cobwebs and dangling debris, hovers the luminous apparition, a mere two or three centimeters in diameter:

> In that single, gigantic instant I saw millions of acts both delightful and awful; not one of them amazed me more than the fact that all of them occupied the same point in space, without overlapping or transparency. What my eyes beheld was simultaneous, but what I shall now write down will be successive, because language is successive. . . . On the dark part of the step toward the right, I saw a small iridescent sphere of almost unbearable brilliance.[6]

By using the Hebrew letter Aleph as the title of his story, Borges stirs his readers' sense of mystery. No specific cabalistic teaching is invoked

---

[5] *Dreamtigers*, trans. Mildred Boyer and Harold Morland (New York, 1970), pp. 44-45.

[6] *The Aleph and Other Stories* (New York, 1971), trans. Norman di Giovanni, in collaboration with author.

in the story. What the image of the Aleph surely shows is that the ubiquitous center and the infinite sphere appear in unexpected literary guises.

Samuel Beckett's works as well are marked by the mysteries surrounding temporality. In *Krapp's Last Tape*, it is the venerable symbol of the "infinite circle" itself which, in the guise of the beloved's eyes, emerges with a hint of its old, transcendent power. The image surfaces for Krapp as he plays his life back to himself, reel by reel. He drunkenly listens to his not-yet-ravaged voice, which allows him to relive a moment of thirty years ago. The taped voice says something about a girl in a rowboat, and Krapp makes convulsive gestures of fascination. His hazy memory requires jogging, so he rewinds the tape to listen once more to his former self: "But under us all moved, and moved us, gently, up and down, and from side to side."[7] Now the moment had become fully present to Krapp. Abruptly he switches off the machine:

> Just been listening to that stupid bastard I took myself for thirty years ago, hard to believe I was ever as bad as that. Thank God that's all done with anyway. [*Pause*] The eyes she had! [*Broods, realizes he is recording silence, switches off, broods. Finally.*] Everything there, everything, all the — [*Realizes this is not being recorded, switches on.*] Everything there, everything on this old muckball, all the light and dark and famine and feasting of . . . [*hesitates*] . . . the ages! [*In a shout.*] Yes![8]

An irretrievable moment of love reaches Krapp from the past when he hears the scratchy playback of the tape. There was meaning in the all-encompassing pinpoint in the eyes of the beloved, perceived in a moment of intense awareness. Krapp listens and reflects on the nauseating impossibility of making his life cohere. The ongoing dialogue between a dissolute present and a vibrant past moment turns out to be a monologue of despair.

---

[7] *Krapp's Last Tape* (London, 1965), p. 20.
[8] *ibid.*, pp. 17-18.

Chapter Eight

EPILOGUE:
IRONY AND THE END OF LITERATURE

> As a man shall not put asunder what God has joined
> together, so neither shall man join together what God has
> put asunder, for such a sickly longing is simply longing to
> have the perfect before its time.
>
> SOREN KIERKEGAARD, *THE CONCEPT OF IRONY*

Among the German philosophers in intellectual proximity to Hegel
and Schelling was one K.W.F. Solger, who pushed to its most radical
conclusion the play with polarities which had long hovered about the
idea of aesthetic beauty. He is scarcely known today, and his contri-
bution to aesthetics still awaits a full evaluation. Solger's definition of
a symbol can be seen to be in essential agreement with Hegel's "sensuous radiance of the idea":

The symbol is actually what it signifies: the idea in its unmediated reality.
The symbol is therefore always true to itself, no mere copy of something true.[1]

He went some distance beyond Hegel, however, when he postulated
that symbols are in fact the entire work of art *in nuce*, and that their
structure is therefore analogous to the work as a whole. This claim —
especially as it applied to literature — was the basis for his remarkable
theory of irony.[2] Like Hegel and others, he saw the confrontation of

---

[1] *Vorlesungen über Aesthetik* (Leipzig, 1829), p. 129. This book was compiled from
students' lecture notes. This and subsequent translations are mine.
[2] See also René Wellek, *A History of Modern Criticism 1750-1950* (New Haven,
1955), II, p. 299.

opposites as an essential feature of the aesthetic object, but by insisting that such a coincidence of polarities is after all only make-believe — an illusion by which no one is deceived — he went considerably beyond his more famous and influential colleagues. It is this provisional — even conspiratorial — acceptance of poetic "truth" which is to Solger the appropriate and necessary stance vis-à-vis the products of literary imagination. It is an "ironic" stance, and understood in that way, irony is the "essential center" and the "unchanging essence" of art on the part of both author and reader.[3] Whereas irony in romantic theory and practice had been, by and large, a certain attitude toward the world, a sensibility reflected in artistic posture and style, it was now advanced as a defining characteristic of the poetic imagination itself. For Solger it was not enough to see irony as "transcendental buffoonery" of the writer, as did Friedrich Schlegel in a memorable aperçu.[4] Instead he stated starkly and without qualification that "without irony there can be no art at all,"[5] thereby giving his remarks, in a certain sense, a peculiarly modern edge. One can discern a spiritual kinship between passages in Camus' famous essay "Rebellion and Art" and Solger's early nineteenth-century ruminations:

From Solger's *Erwin*:

And we can hardly doubt the possibility [of such a fundamental irony] since we have become convinced that this unchanging essence can be present only where there is also the nothingness of real existence. Because art, even while constructing a concrete existence, can always dissolve it with its accompanying irony.[6]

From Camus' "Rebellion and Art":

In every rebellion is to be found the metaphysical demand for unity, the impossibility of capturing it, and the construction of a substitute universe. Rebellion, from this point of view, is a fabricator of universes. This also defines art.[7]

It behooves us also, in this connection, to consider the emphasis on irony in Cleanth Brooks' critical position which became one of the important tenets in American New Criticism of the early postwar

---

[3] *Erwin, Vier Gespräche über das Schöne in der Kunst* (Berlin, 1907), p. 391.

[4] *Friedrich Schlegel 1794-1804: seine prosaischen Jugendschriften*, ed. Jakob Minor (Vienna, 1882), p. 182.

[5] *Vorlesungen über Aesthetik* (Leipzig, 1829), p. 199.

[6] *Erwin*, p. 392.

[7] *The Rebel*, trans. Anthony Bower (New York, 1956), p. 225.

period. Irony results from the paradox which Brooks saw residing at the heart of poetic discourse. He was able to point to it even in the verses of a poet like Wordsworth who "usually prefers a direct attack."[8] In Brooks we find little abstract speculation regarding the fusion — in poetry — between the universal and the particular, and no theory at all dealing with poetic attempts to reconcile non-temporal ideas with time-bound actuality. But by building on his vast experience with literature, as well as on his analytic skill and sensitivity, he came to recognize that some form of paradoxicality — as well as the irony resulting from it — were inherent in the nature of poetic discourse:

> There is a sense in which all such well wrought urns [in Shakespeare's "The Phoenix and the Turtle," in John Donne's "Canonization," and in Keats' "Ode to a Grecian Urn"] contain the ashes of a Phoenix. The urns are not meant for memorial purposes only, though that often seems to be their chief significance to the professors of literature. The phoenix rises from its ashes or ought to rise; but it will not arise for all our mere sifting and measuring the ashes, or testing them for their chemical content. *We must be prepared to accept the paradox of the imagination itself*; else "Beautie, Truth, and Raritie" [referring to Shakespeare's poem] remain enclosed in their cinders and we shall end with essential cinders, for all our pain.[9]

The numerous subdivisions of ironic styles or modes, such as romantic and dramatic irony, the irony of satire, ironic understatement or ironic hyperbole — all these are not up for discussion in our context.[10] However, one attribute which can be seen to underlie them all is of direct relevance to our present exploration: the tension existing between opposing elements within the compass of a particular verbal complex. If the irony is satirical, then what is *said* is merely used as a springboard for what is *meant*. There is no room for doubt or hesitancy regarding the intended meaning of, say, Swift's *Modest Proposal*. And if the irony is "dramatic," then there should be a gap — presumably filled with an electric charge — between the information possessed by the protagonist and that assumed to be available to other characters, or to the audience. When the messenger comes to bring Oedipus the news that his "father," King Polybus of Corinth, was not murdered — as prophesied by the oracle — but had died a natural death, Oedipus' triumph is short-lived

---

[8] Cleanth Brooks, *The Well Wrought Urn: Studies in the Structure of Poetry* (New York, 1947), p. 3.

[9] *Ibid.*, p. 21. Italics are mine.

[10] For recent explorations of irony in literature, see Lilian Furst, *Fictions of Romantic Irony* (Cambridge, Mass., 1984). Also Charles I. Glicksberg, *The Ironic Vision in Modern Literature* (The Hague, 1969); D.C. Muecke, *The Compass of Irony* (London, 1969); Wayne C. Booth, *A Rhetoric of Irony* (Chicago, 1974).

and based on ignorance. Here the irony is at least twofold: first, in the predicament of the greatest problem-solver in Thebes, King Oedipus, who unlike the simple herdsman who reared him, is unable to see the deadly net in which he is irreparably entangled, and second, in the situation of the spectators who are privy to the dreadful truth to which Oedipus is still blind.

Within the large compass of ironic modes is one in which the arc of tension holds the two polar forces in precarious equipoise. No sooner does a meaning appear to stabilize, than it jumps — in playful ambivalence — to its complement on the opposite side. The reader cannot decide with finality whether Hans Castorp's raised temperature is a mere physiological response to the tubercle bacillus, or whether it signals a heightening of the entire panoply of his growing spiritual powers. In *The Magic Mountain*, Mann ironically joins the indignities of physical infirmity to the grandeur of an encompassing spirit. Ambivalence and a concomitant lack of dependability as citizens are especially characteristic of Mann's artist figures. They all have something in them of Tonio Kröger who cannot dance like his blond and blue-eyed classmates, or of Gustav Aschenbach, the exemplary artificer who, after a lifetime of steely self-control, is drawn into the Dionysian abyss. But the deck of cards has been well shuffled since Plato: Socrates' poets were ignorant; as mere imitators they were twice removed from the prototypal reality of forms. Mann's artists, on the contrary, are possessors of forbidden knowledge. They are marked men, not because they know too little, but because they know too much.

We might also reach for the most adequate interpretation of Meursault's crime in Camus' *The Stranger*. Is it that which follows from the protagonist's answer to the question of why he killed the Arab: "because of the sun"? Or should we accept the prosecuting attorney's carefully wrought picture of a hardened criminal?

For that matter, is Miss Raby's "eternal moment" in E.M. Forster's story ludicrous or sublime? Or indeed, if we grant the sublimity, is it enhanced or tainted by the presence of its opposite to which it may skip over at any moment?

Such ironic instability is difficult to handle, but at its best it provides a welcome spaciousness, an atmosphere of "play" (like the "play" built into an otherwise close-fitting mechanism) which allows the object of contemplation room and scope for its unfolding. In Beda Alleman's view, this type of irony may effectively counteract an author's sense of manipulative superiority. It is a loving kind of relationship between the author and his material, one capable of bringing about a "relaxed sufficiency" and a "translucency,"[11] not otherwise obtainable.

---

[11] Freely transposed from the German words *Gelöstheit* and *Durchlichtetheit* in Beda Alleman, *Ironie und Dichtung* (Pfullingen, 1956), p. 10.

Solger's position on irony serves to clear the air of multiple and nebulous qualifications and subcategories. For him, irony is one of the defining features of literature, situated at precise coordinates in the human consciousness: at the point of transition where the idea is transmuted into its objectification. From here the irony of art in general — and of literature in particular — radiates into the work. It is an intrinsically "tragic" irony — though not in the Aristotelian sense — and it evokes a feeling of melancholy, regardless of whether a given work is a tragedy or a comedy. Here is how Solger pinpoints the instant of artistic creation: "This moment of transition during which the idea itself is annihilated by reason of the imperfection of all sensible objects . . . is the true seat of art."[12] Contemplation of phenomenal, or earthly, beauty, in Solger's philosophy, is the nearest that we as human beings can come to the apprehension of the absolute idea of beauty. When a sculpture, or a painting, or a poem, strikes us as beautiful, we are also necessarily face to face with earthly imperfection, decay and mortality. As Solger puts it:

> Man's destiny in general and the fact that he partakes of the highest ideas
> and yet must exist [as a mortal being], evokes a genuine feeling of tragedy.
> Man feels his nothingness when he undertakes to embody an absolute idea
> and when he realizes that he can do so only in the midst of the contradictions
> of his existence. Hence it is the imprisonment of man in his human existence
> that is the ground for tragedy.[13]

Solger's relentless anlysis leads to the unresolvable paradox that the only means by which the idea can manifest itself, must also lead to the annihilation of that idea.

In our time irony has invaded the phenomenon of language itself. The abyss which lies just beyond an articulated world is shown as both beckoning and forbidding. Modern writers delight in driving a wedge between words and their lexical meanings and thus creating an ironic tension between sound and sense. Caught in that situation, language can no longer be depended on as representative of preexisting meanings, but is more likely perceived as a system which for ages has been used — especially by the poets — to impose meanings on an inchoate world.

---

[12] "Dieser Augenblick des Übergangs nun, in dem die Idee selbst notwendig zunichte wird, muß der wahre Sitz der Kunst . . . sein" (*Erwin*, p. 387).

[13] "Das Loos des Menschen überhaupt, dass er an dem Höchsten Theil hat und dennoch existieren muß, bringt das echt tragische Gefühl hervor. Der Mensch fühlt seine Nichtigkeit, wenn er die Idee darstellen will und dies nur in den Widersprüchen der Existenz vermag. Das Gebanntsein des Menschen in die Existenz also ist es, wodurch das tragische Gefühl erregt wird" (*Vorlesungen über Ästhetik*, reprint of 1829 edition. Darmstadt, 1980, p. 97).

No doubt the exposure to chaos can bring about a vertiginous intoxication, and the insights that such temporarily disorienting trips may yield, are tolerable only — at least within the confines of sanity — so long as traditional and ingrained verbal habits have not slipped beyond reach. Protected by the armor of words, the writer, in conspiracy with the reader, will indulge in a bravado display of virtuosity, cling spread-eagled to a *double* or *triple entendre*, only to feel more keenly the pressure of chaos. In sum, the charge of linguistic subversion might well be added to the venerable Platonic list of accusations against the poets.

Contemporary writing typically raises questions about its own legitimacy. Joyce's *Ulysses* and Mann's *Doctor Faustus* are sometimes invoked as novels written to mark the end of a genre. And beyond these lies the even more radically self-defeating gleam of the candle in the "cathedral scene" of Kafka's *Trial*, which "actually increases the darkness." Finally, there is the gesture of total paralysis in thirty seconds of proceedings devised by Samuel Beckett, where a stage strewn with debris is visited by two identical whimpers, each "vagitus" framed by audible in- and exhalations and by synchronized brightenings and darkenings of lights.[14] The irony of ambivalence here seems to have reached the dead end of incurable paralysis.

At the opposite end of such representation of emptiness lies the "fulfilled moment." The fusion between the concretely temporal and the abstractly eternal makes for a new amalgam which is no longer reducible to its components. In the absolute moment, existence and meaning are one. In the absence of separations and oppositions, there can be no irony. The fulfilled moment can refer only to itself, an observation which — coming full circle — can be made about the empty moment as well.

To a religious thinker like Kierkegaard, the constant intrusion of infinity in the writings of German Romantics was to condemned. Such fantasies, he felt, only served to "hollow out actuality." It was moreover a "cowardly, effeminate ruse for speaking oneself out of the world."[15] When Kierkegaard stated that "actuality acquires its validity through action," he is reminiscent of Goethe, and it was not surprisingly Goethe whom he praised for having unromantically "succeeded in making his existence as a poet congrue with his actuality," a process which allowed the poet to "master" his irony. The irony of Romanticism, in Kierkegaard's view, is not mastered.[16] A typically romantic production is "either a darling with which the Romanticist is wholly infatuated and

---

[14] *First Love and Other Shorts* (New York: Grove Press 1974), p. 89.

[15] Soren Kierkegaard, *The Concept of Irony, with Constant Reference to Socrates*, trans. Lee Capel (New York, 1964), p. 337.

[16] For Kierkegaard's concept of "mastered irony," see *ibid*.

which he is unable to explain how it has been possible to call to life, or it is an object of disgust."[17] He disapproved of both mysticism and Romanticism as facile shortcuts to salvation:

> As a man shall not put asunder what God has joined together, so neither shall man join together what God has put asunder, for such a sickly longing is simply longing to have the perfect before its time.[18]

The welding of the particular and the general, of the actual and the conceptual, into a seamless union takes place on the far side of Kierkegaard's "leap into faith." There the all-encompassing point exists as a vision, free of metaphor and indirection, cleansed of irony and apprehended in an instant. Its realization would mark the end of literature.

---

[17] *Ibid.*
[18] *Ibid.*, p. 341.

BIBLIOGRAPHY

Abrams, M.H. *The Mirror and the Lamp.* New York, 1953.
Alleman, Beda. *Ironie und Dichtung.* Pfullingen, 1956.
Aristotle's Theory of Poetry and Fine Arts. Trans. S.H. Butcher. New York, 1951.
Auerbach, Erich. *Dante, Poet of the Secular World.* Chicago, 1961.
——. *Scenes from the Drama of European Literature.* New York, 1959.
Baeumker, Clemens. "Das pseudo-hermetische Buch der 24 Meister (liber XXIV philosophorum)." In *Studien und Charakteristiken zur Geschichte der Philosophie, insbesondere des Mittelalters.* Münster, 1927.
Beckett, Samuel. *First Love and Other Stories.* New York, 1974.
——. *Krapp's Last Tape.* London, 1968.
Beja, Morris. *Epiphany in the Modern Novel.* Seattle, 1971.
Bergson, Henri. *Time and Free Will: An Essay on the Immediate Data of Consciousness.* 1889. New York, 1960.
Bergsten, Gunilla. *Thomas Mann's Doctor Faustus: The Sources and Structure of the Novel.* Chicago, 1969.
Blake William. *The Complete Writings of William Blake.* Ed. Geoffrey Keynes. London, 1964.
Bonner, Campbell. *Studies in Amulets, Chiefly Graeco-Egyptian.* Ann Arbor, 1950.
Booth, Wayne C. *A Rhetoric of Irony.* Chicago, 1974.
Borges, Jorge Luis. *The Aleph and Other Stories, 1933-1969.* New York, 1971.
——. *Other Inquisitions, 1937-1952.* New York, 1965.
——. *Dreamtigers.* New York, 1964.
Brooks, Cleanth. *The Well Wrought Urn: Studies in the Structure of Poetry.* New York, 1947.
Brown, Calvin S. "The Entomological Source of Mann's Poisonous Butterfly." *Germanic Review,* 37 (January 1962), 116-120.
Bruno, Giordano. *Opere di Giordano Bruno e di Tommaso Campanella.* Eds. Amerio and Guzzo. Milano, 1956.

Camus, Albert. *The Rebel.* Trans. Anthony Bower. New York, 1956.
———. *The Myth of Sisyphus and Other Stories.* Trans. Justin O'Brien. New York, 1955.
Cassirer, Ernst. *The Individual and the Cosmos in Renaissance Philosophy.* Trans. Mario Donati. New York, 1963.
Cornwall, Ethel. *The 'Still Point.'* New Brunswick, N.J., 1962.
Crawshaw, Richard. *The Poems of Richard Crawshaw.* Ed. L.C. Martin. Oxford, 1966.
Cusanus, Nicolas (Nikolaus von Kues). *Werke.* Ed. Paul Wilpert. 2 vols. Berlin, 1967.
——— (Nicholas of Cusa). *The Vision of God.* Trans. Emma G. Salter. New York, 1960.
———. *Of Learned Ignorance.* Trans. Germain Heron. New Haven, 1954.
———. *La Divina Commedia.* Ed. Scartazzini. Milano, 1951.
———. *Opere di Dante.* Ed. E. Moore. Oxford, 1924.
Denifle, H. and F. Ehrle. *Archiv für Literatur- und Kirchengeschichte des Mittelalters.* 1886. Vol. II.
Dieckmann, Liselotte. *Hieroglyphics.* St. Louis, 1970.
Diels, H. and W. Kranz. *Die Fragmente der Vorsokratiker.* 5th ed. Berlin, 1934.
Eliot, T.S. *Selected Essays.* New York, 1950.
Emrich, Wilhelm. *Die Symbolik von Faust II.* Bonn, 1957.
Forster, E.M. *The Collected Tales of E.M. Forster.* New York, 1947.
———. *Virginia Woolf.* New York, 1942.
Fraisse, Paul. *The Psychology of Time.* London, 1964.
Frank, Joseph. "Reaction as Progress: Thomas Mann's *Dr. Faustus.*" In *The Widening Gyre.* New Brunswick, N.J., 1963.
Friedrich, Hugo (ed.) *Dante Alghieri: Aufsätze zur Divina Commedia.* Darmstadt, 1978.
Frye, Northrop. "The Road to Excess." In *Myth and Symbol.* Ed. Bernice Slote. Lincoln, Neb., 1963.
Furst, Lilian R. *Fictions of Romantic Irony.* Cambridge, Mass., 1984.
Gentile, Giovanni. *Il pensiero del rinascimento.* Florence, 1940.
Glicksberg, Charles I. *The Ironic Vision in Modern Literature.* The Hague, 1969.
Goethe, Johann W. von. *Goethes Werke: Hamburger Ausgabe.* Ed. Erich Trunz. Hamburg, 1956.
———. *Jubiläumsausgabe.* Stuttgart and Berlin, 1902-1912.
Graham, John. "Time in the Novels of Virginia Woolf." *University of Toronto Quarterly,* 28 (1948), 186-201.
Guiguet, Jean. *Virginia Woolf and Her Works.* New York, 1965.
Guardini, Romano. "Die Ordnung des Seins und der Bewegung." In *Dante Alighieri: Aufsätze zur Divina Commedia.* Ed. Hugo Friedrich. Darmstadt, 1968.

Hartley, Lodwick. "Of Time and Virginia Woolf." *Sewanee Review*, 47 (1939), 235-241.

Hegel, G.W.F. *Jubiläumsausgabe*. Ed. Hermann Glockner. Stuttgart, 1964. Vol. XII.

Heidegger, Martin. *Sein und Zeit*. Halle a.d.S., 1929.

Hollander, Robert. *Allegory in Dante's 'Commedia.'* Princeton, 1969.

Horapollo. *The Hieroglyphics of Horapollo*. Trans. George Boas. New York, 1950.

Hulme, T.E. *Speculations: Essays on Humanism and the Philosophy of Art*. Ed. Herbert Read. London, 1954.

Kermode, Frank. *The Sense of an Ending: Studies in the Theory of Fiction*. New York, 1966.

Kierkegaard, Soren. *The Concept of Irony, with Constant Reference to Socrates*. Trans. Lee Capel. New York, 1964.

Kleist, Heinrich von. "Über das Marionettentheater." In *Sämtliche Werke und Briefe*. Ed. Helmut Sembdner. Munich, 1964.

Klett, Ada. *Der Streit um Faust II seit 1900*. Jena, 1961.

Koyré Alexandre. *From the Closed World to the Infinite Universe*. Baltimore, 1957.

Krieger, Murray. "The Ekphrastic Principle and the Still Movement of Poetry: Laokoon Revisited." In *The Play and Place of Criticism*. Baltimore, 1967.

Mahnke, Dietrich. *Unendliche Sphäre und Allmittelpunkt*. Deutsche Vierteljahresschrift, Bücherreihe no. 23. Halle, 1937.

Mann, Thomas. *Doctor Faustus: The Life of the German Composer Adrian Leverkühn as Told by a Friend*. Trans. H.D. Lowe-Porter. New York, 1960.

——. *Doktor Faustus: Das Leben des deutschen Tonsetzers Adrian Leverkühn, erzählt von einem Freunde*. Frankfurt, 1960.

——. *Die Entstehung des Doktor Faustus*. Amsterdam, 1960.

——. *Stories of Three Decades*. Trans. H.T. Lowe-Porter. New York, 1955.

——. *The Story of a Novel: The Genesis of Doctor Faustus*. Trans. R. and C. Winston. New York, 1961.

——. *Der Zauberberg*. 4th ed. Berlin and Frankfurt, 1960.

Mendilow, A.A. *Time and the Novel*. London, 1952.

Meyerhoff, Hans. *Time in Literature*. Berkeley, 1960.

Muecke, D.C. *The Compass of Irony*. London, 1969.

Naremore, James. *The World Without a Self*. New Haven, 1973.

Olschki, L. "Giordano Bruno." *Deutsche Vierteljahresschrift für Literaturwissenschaft und Geistesgeschichte*, 2 (1924), 1-78.

Panofsky, Erwin. *Studies in Iconography*. New York, 1970.

Pascal, Blaise. *Pensées et opuscules*. Ed. M. Léon Brunschvicg. Paris, 1952.

Plotinus. *Enneads.* Trans. Stephen Mackenna. 5 vols. London, 1926-1930.
Politzer, Heinz. "The Tree of Knowledge and the Sin of Science: Vegetarian Symbols in Goethe's *Faust.*" In *Aspects of the Eighteenth Century.* Ed. Earl R. Wasserman. Baltimore, 1965.
Poulet, Georges. *The Metamorphoses of the Circle.* Baltimore, 1966.
——. *Studies in Human Time.* Trans. Elliott Coleman. Baltimore, 1956.
Pound, Ezra. *Pavannes and Divisions.* New York, 1918.
Richter, Harvena. *Virginia Woolf: The Inward Voyage.* Princeton, 1970.
Salaman, Esther. *A Collection of Moments.* London, 1970.
Salm, Peter. "Pinpoint of Eternity: The Sufficient Moment in Literature." *Studies in Eighteenth-Century Culture*, 3 (1973).
——. *The Poem as Plant: A Biological View of Goethe's Faust.* Cleveland, 1971.
Sartre, Jean-Paul. *Nausea.* Trans. Lloyd Alexander. New York, 1964.
Schlegel, Friedrich. *Friedrich Schlegel: Seine prosaischen Jugendschriften.* Ed. Jakob Minor. 2 vols. Vienna, 1882.
Scott, Walter. *Hermetica.* 2 vols. Oxford, 1924.
Shattuck, Roger. *The Banquet Years.* Rev. ed. New York, 1972.
Singleton, Charles S. *Commedia: Elements of Structure.* Cambridge, 1954.
——. "Vita Nuova XII: Love's Obscure Words." *Romanic Review*, 36 (1945), 89-102.
Solger, K.W.F. *Nachgelassene Schriften und Briefwechsel.* Eds. Tieck and Raumer. 2 vols. Heidelberg, 1973.
——. *Erwin: Vier Gespräche über das Schöne und die Kunst.* Ed. Wolfgang Henckmann. Munich, 1971.
——. *Vorlesungen über Aesthetik.* Ed. K.L. Heyse. Darmstadt, 1969.
Tillich, Paul. "The Eternal Now." In *The Eternal Now.* New York, 1963.
Vossler, Karl. "Dante als religiöser Dichter." In *Dante Alighieri: Aufsätze zur Divina Commedia.* Ed. Hugo Friedrich. Darmstadt, 1968.
Walzel, Oskar. "Tragik bei Solger." *Helicon* (Amsterdam, 1940), 27-49.
——. "Methode? Ironie bei Fr. Schlegel und bei Solger." In *Helicon* (Amsterdam, 1938), 33-50.
Weigand, Hermann J. "Wetten und Pakte in Goethes *Faust.*" *Monatshefte*, 53 (December 1961), 325-337.
——. *Thomas Mann's Novel 'Der Zauberberg.'* New York, 1933.
Wellek, René. *A History of Modern Criticism 1750-1950.* New Haven, 1955. Vol. II.
—— and Austin Warren. *Theory of Literature.* 2nd ed. New York, 1956.
Wheelwright, Phillip. *Metaphor and Reality.* Bloomington, 1964.

Wiget, Eric. *Virginia Woolf und die Konzeption der Zeit in ihren Werken.* Diss., Zurich, 1949.

Wimsatt, W.K., Jr. "The Concrete Universal." In *The Verbal Icon.* New York, 1958.

Wilson, James S. "Time and Virginia Woolf." *The Virginia Quarterly Review*, 18 (1942), 267-276.

Woolf, Virginia. *Between the Acts.* New York, 1941.

———. *The Common Reader.* London, 1925.

———. *Mrs. Dalloway.* New York, 1925.

———. *A Haunted House and Other Short Stories.* New York, 1944.

———. *The Moment and Other Essays.* New York, 1948.

———. *Moments of Being.* Ed. Jeanne Schulkind. New York, 1976.

———. *Night and Day.* New York, 1920.

———. *Orlando: A Biography.* New York, 1956.

———. *To the Lighthouse.* New York, 1927.

———. *The Waves.* New York, 1931.

———. *A Writer's Diary.* Ed. Leonard Woolf. New York, 1954.

Yates, Frances. *Giordano Bruno and the Hermetic Tradition.* London, 1964.

Young, Edward. *Conjectures on Original Composition.* Ed. E.K. Morley. Manchester, 1918.

Ziolkowski, Theodore. "James Joyces Epiphanie und die Überwindung der empirischen Welt in der modernen deutschen Prosa." *Deutsche Vierteljahresschrift*, 35 (1961), 594-616.

INDEX OF NAMES

Peter Salm is Professor of Comparative Literature and German at Case Western Reserve University. As an undergraduate at UCLA he studied Astronomy and German. After a three-year stint in the New York publishing industry, he enrolled at Yale, where he received his doctorate under René Wellek's directorship. Salm's translation of Goethe's *Faust 1* is published by Bantam. His other books are *Three Modes of Criticism* (1968) and *The Poem as Plant: A Biological View of Goethe's **Faust*** (1971).